THE

MISSIONARY CRUSADE

AGAINST

STATE EDUCATION

IN

INDIA.

"Thus, duties rising out of good possess'd,
And prudent caution needful to avert
Impending evil, equally require
That the whole people should be taught and train'd."

WORDSWORTH.

BY

A NATIVE OF SOUTHERN INDIA.

Madras.

1883.

THE

MISSIONARY CRUSADE

AGAINST

STATE EDUCATION

IN

INDIA.

"Thus, duties rising out of good possess'd,
And prudent caution needful to avert
Impending evil, equally require
That the whole people should be taught and train'd."

WORDSWORTH.

BY

A NATIVE OF SOUTHERN INDIA.

————➤●●◄————

𝔐𝔞𝔡𝔯𝔞𝔰.

1883.

THE
MISSIONARY CRUSADE.

———◦◦❀◦◦———

It cannot be denied that the present is a most critical moment for the cause of Education in India; and there are reasons for thinking that the unfortunate differences which exist, urged on in the way and to the extent which they have been, are likely to terminate in results far from satisfactory, and even such as to upset all the educational Work of nearly half a century. The grave evils that would certainly spring from the success of the Missionary agitation against the maintenance of the State connection with Higher Education are so great that it is necessary to counteract them; and it is most important that the Education Commission and the Viceregal Council, as well as the public both here and in England, should have laid before them all relevant facts and the convictions and feelings of the people of the country as to the manner in which, and agency whereby their children shall be educated, and thus should have the means of forming a correct judgment, before they are misled to join in the persistent missionary crusade against the enlightened policy to which the marked improvement of late years in the education of all classes in India is mainly attributable. It is from no desire "to prejudge and oppose the action of the Viceregal Commission," as certain missionary agents are ready to insinuate when any one ventures to raise his voice on this subject, that we publish the following remarks—our aim is simply to enquire into the real meaning and motive of the agitation set on foot by a powerful missionary faction against the existing educational plans of the Government, and solemnly appeal to every responsible Statesman in India and England and every unprejudiced Member of the Education Commission, entreating each one to pause ere he allows himself to be carried away by the repeated utterances of these missionaries, and thus imperils by his vote the very foundations of our well tried educational structure and the best means of promoting the general progress and enlightenment of the country.

I.   It is claimed by the Missionaries, and we have no wish to contest the claim, that the appointment of the Education Commission was brought about by the Missionary agitation, especially in Madras.   The inference as to what must be expected from it by its promoters is only too obvious.

(a)   In the *Free Church Monthly* of the 1st June 1882, (p. 177) the following passage occurs :—

"Early in April the Rev. W. Miller returned from Calcutta to Madras, after having done noble service in the cause of Christian and independent education as a Member of the Government of India's Commission, which has closed its first session of inquiry.   He writes most hopefully of the effect of this inquiry, *which, more than any other, he has brought about, * * * * *.*"   "I (Mr. Miller) did not press our Madras grievances.   They are known in a general way, to the members of the Commission, *and it is tolerably well-known how large a share they had in the formation of the Commission.*"

(b)   The following passage occurs in the *Madras Mail* of the 11th March 1882 :—

"We were recently informed by telegraph from Calcutta that 'the Council of Education in England and several important Missionary bodies formally accuse the Indian Department of Public Instruction of having diverted an undue share of public money from the general education of the people at large to the over-education of a small and favored class.'   This confirms our previous suspicions as to the origin of the Educational Commission.   The action of the Government has been instigated by certain religious bodies in England, moved thereto by their agents in this country. The Missionary bodies have some resemblance to the Manchester manufacturers. They have the same perseverance: they bring the same sort of pressure to bear on Viceroy and Secretaries of State; and they have been crowned at last with the same success. There is also the same want of frankness in the main plea they put forward. Both place the hardship to the poor in the front of their complaint. Without stopping to inquire how far this is sincere on the part of the manufacturers, we may say that this zeal for the education of the masses comes strangely from the lips of men whose efforts have chiefly been given to the higher education, and who are now turning out from their schools nearly as many over educated men as the government institutions. It is not quite ingenuous of the missionary societies to attack the higher education at the very time when they are striving to extend their own operations, and to get the whole of this kind of work into their own hands; nor can we say that the Supreme Government have been perfectly frank in making no mention of the power behind them at whose instigation they are acting. The Government speak in their resolution of handing over their schools and colleges to groups of native gentlemen. But these are only stalking horses. Behind them are the missionary bodies, waiting till the moment comes to declare themselves. Our chief concern, however, is not with nice points of conduct, but with a broad policy. Government, it is supposed, are now about to surrender into private hands one important part of their own duty, and we have now to see if those who undertake the work have the means to carry it out, and have such a prospect of permanency that Government can safely leave it in their hands."

II. The self-styled and self-constituted "General Council on Education in India," while disclaiming in express terms to be " identified with any party," is nothing but a clique of restless agitators for the overthrow of national, and the spread of missionary, education; for we hesitate to apply the name Christian to a system of education which is a libel on Christianity, and whose advancement is being at the present moment promoted by an agitation of " a hollow, selfish and unprincipled character." (Dr. Duncan's evidence before the Commission at Madras, page 25.)

The " General Council" published in the early part of 1882, " for private circulation," a pamphlet, which we shall hereafter, for the sake of brevity, refer to as the *Secret Pamphlet*, entitled " Answers to Queries on the working of the Educational Despatch of 1854, sent out by the General Council on Education in India." It consists of (1) An introductory note signed by a person now notorious in India in connexion with educational agitations, the Rev. James Johnston, (2) A list of Queries, (3) Answers to Queries, (4) An Appendix, Pages 1—29 are occupied with the answers of missionaries and missionary-schoolmasters, all, of course, hostile to Government Institutions. Pages 30—38 deal with answers to queries which are thus spoken of in an introductory note :—

" The four papers which follow are of special interest, and with one exception of great value as coming from a class of men from whom we should not presume to solicit answers to our unofficial inquiries, and whose personal interests and prepossessions would naturally be on the side of the order of things by which they have risen and through which they must rise higher. We give them with much satisfaction as samples of not a few in their position, only wishing that more had reached us, while grateful that even these have spoken so freely out. Nothing but deep conviction and a generous impulse could have led three of these gentlemen to rise so far above official reserve and the influences of their order, and speak out as they have done. As for the other, who has favoured us with the routine view with which official reports are filled, we let him speak for himself as an average example of his class."

The reader will at once perceive the humour of such an utterance by an association which " neither originated with, nor represents the missionary societies labouring in India" (Secret Pamphlet, p. ii) and which "is not identified with any party"(Id. p. iii). The unfortunate gentleman " who has favoured us with the routine view with which official reports are filled" is " a Professor in a Government College" (Secret Pamphlet, p.35), who, having honestly stated his views on the different points upon which the "Council" thirsted for knowledge, which are the views of more than nine-tenths of those who have the good of India and its millions at heart, is thus denounced, simply because he did not fall in with the missionary proclivities of this so-called " Council," which " is not identified with any party," and which does not "represent the missionary societies labouring in India." The Appendix opens with the following words :—" Besides the formal answers to the queries sent, we have received many communications, both public and private, of great importance, bearing on this question, from which we subjoin a few extracts." (N.B.—Purely missionary evidence is given *in extenso*). We have then a sort of paraphrase or abstract of a statement " of much value" by the Director of Public Instruction, Bengal; but what the real value of the abstract is, it is utterly impossible to say, as H. H. the Maharajah of Travancore has but recently very clearly shown*, and the Governor of Madras, in his letter to His Highness, published in the same pamphlet, is of the same opinion, that Mr. Johnston's manipulation of statements not quite favourable to his own views is apt to be influenced by these views, and that, therefore, his representations of other people's views are perfectly worthless as showing what others think, and absolutely inadmissible as proof of any fact of this kind, be it what it may. Allusion is then made to " several public documents" sent by Dr. Leitner of Lahore. We have next an extract from a letter addressed by Mr. Grigg, Director of Public Instruction, Madras, to the Local Government, recommending an increased grant to the Christian College, which having been refused, of course, constitutes a grievance in the eyes

---

* In a pamphlet entitled " A Cursory Notice of certain statements in the Rev. James Johnston's Reply," to his Highness's letter to the Governor of Madras.

of the "Council" (not identified with any party) and its irrepressible Honorary Secretary. Then we have the following statement :—

"Partiality in the Education Department comes out in other matters than grants-in-aid. Take, as an illustration, the composition of the University of Madras, on which much of the character of education depends.

(1) The Wesleyan Mission, the London Mission, the German and American Missions are quite unrepresented in the University, though all do something, and the two first an immense deal in education. (2.) Of the 93 members of the Senate, all but 25 are Government servants and even some of these 25 are more or less bound to Government. (Of course many of the Government servants are capital men). (3.) Of the 93, 22 are directly and distinctly in the Government Education Department, and only 13 are in any way at all (many of them very indirectly) representatives of aided education. (4.) In the Presidency College there are eight professors and assistant professors; in the Christian College there are seven. I don't think there is a man in Madras who would say that the *eight* are superior to the *seven* in academic rank or in any way more distinguished : yet out of the *eight* no less than *seven* are members of the Senate, out of the *seven* only *two*. This, we think, would not be tolerated in Calcutta or Bombay."*

It will be observed that in this extract, this Council which is not identified with anybody, and which represents itself as the champion of *all* education independent of Government, is here, as everywhere throughout the Secret Pamphlet, concerned only about the supposed grievances of certain missionary bodies, anxious that they and they alone should have the supreme control of education in India.

Here, then, is a pamphlet of 41 pages and four pages of an introduction, professedly put forth to further the principles laid down in the Despatch of 1854. Nineteen-twentieths of the pamphlet is devoted to tirades against Government schools by missionaries, and one witness, who ventures to defend them, is de-

---

* This misleading statement is fully answered by Dr. W. H. Wilson in his Evidence and Cross-Examination before the Education Commission.

nounced in a most ungentlemanly and uncalled for manner. No one, at least so the pamphlet hints, can speak the truth on the subject of Indian education except missionaries. In these circumstances, we confidently ask the unbiased reader to judge of the sincerity and ingenuousness of the following statement :—

"The Council on Education is not identified with any party. We are, from conviction based on experience, in favour of carrying out the principles of the Despatch of 1854, as being the best for the present condition of Society in India. We take our stand on that Despatch, as from the first the declared policy of the Government, though it has never had a fair and full trial, but which has whenever tried, proved by results its adaptation to the wants of the country. (Secret Pamphlet, p. iii).

From the facts we have stated it is abundantly clear, that this so-called " Council" is a body working in behalf of missionary education in India.

The Rev. J. Johnston, in his letter to the Maharajah of Travancore, in which he professes to explain the aims of the " Council," says :—"We have been misrepresented as seeking the transference of Government Colleges to missionary societies." Let the Rev. J. Johnston speak for himself. In his pamphlet, " Our Educational Policy in India," second edition, 1880, the following passages occur, (pp. 42— 43) :—

"We have had noble examples of liberality among the natives of India in both building and endowing colleges and schools before Government began to do it for them.

" We do not expect them to volunteer to do this; like most subjects of an absolute Government, they prefer to have everything done for them. But if left alone in a firm, cautious, and friendly spirit, they could and would provide it for themselves.

" But would this be an advantage in a missionary point of view ? That is not with me the first question. Is it right in itself ? That is what we have to see to ; and if it is right, I am sure it will be best for the righteous cause.

" Missions have nothing to fear in a fair competition with natives of any class. It is only the unfair competition with a Government, backed by the prestige and pay that makes voluntary efforts by either natives or missions so arduous or impossible. If that competition were withdrawn, we have reason to believe that colleges would soon cease to be a burden on the funds of the Church. They would, with slightly higher fees and a larger attendance, pay their own expenses. The average attendance at aided colleges is only seventy-four; they could educate three or four times that number without any corresponding addition to their contributions *from home.** If any should still say that the Natives of India could not or would not support colleges for themselves, I would only say, that in that improbable and sad case they would have themselves to blame, and could not charge on Government the fault of aiding either missionary societies or European residents in providing the needed means of education."

Again at pp. 54—55 the pamphlet is concluded thus : —

" There will be opposition, there may be a conflict, imperiling our rule, if not our existence, in the country, ere that triumph is attained, but it will come, and it will, we believe, come with a sudden and mighty rush which will startle and amaze an incredulous age. Hinduism is like no other system that now exists, or has ever existed in the world. It seems as if it would defy those processes of disintegration, by which believers may be gathered by units or tens or hundreds from other sects and races, in other systems, in other lands, or even in India, as among the aboriginal tribes, or those simpler races in Tinnevelly and Travancore, which never fully partook of the fatal privileges of Brahminical religion, and were never brought within the iron bondage of caste, where Missions have been so largely successful. Hinduism defies the tooth of time and the tool of the engineer to disintegrate it, or to pick out a stone from the hard and compact structure, except in a few rare and exceptional cases, and the intensity of passion with which these few conversions are felt and resented shows how perfect is the unity of the body—" If one member suffers all the members suffer with it." When Hinduism falls, it will fall as those grand old towers fall which have outlived the age and state of society for which they were constructed ; so strongly cemented that they will stand or fall entire—they cannot be taken down like our frail modern structures, stone by stone.

" It is only by the slow and persevering process of sapping and mining that they can be brought to the ground, and they fall in one solid mass. It is thus that this great donjon, in which superstition and caste have kept the millions of India as

---

* Mr. Johnston, therefore, is, clearly only referring to Missionary Colleges, and not Native Institutions for the development of which Messrs. Johnston and Miller have recently begun to manifest such a marvellous zeal.

in a castle of despair, will one day fall, " to rise no more at all.'
A thousand agencies are at work to undermine it, secular and
religious, and we wish them all God-speed ; but none can compare with the full and clear proclamation of the glorious gospel
in thoroughly equipped and efficiently conducted educational
institutions, in which Divine light is thrown on every subject of
human study, by generous and disinterested men of the highest
culture and Christian character."

Now, we shall presently prove by unimpeachable
evidence that natives would not at present found
Colleges of their own, and the Rev. J. Johnston knows
the fact as well as we do. If the quotations above
given be read in the light of this fact, what, we
should like to know, becomes of the ingenuousness
either of the Rev. James Johnston, or of the so-called
" Council on Education" which he represents?

The *Hindu Patriot,* in dealing with the *Queries,*
the answers to which form the principal portion of
the contents of the Secret Pamphlet, hits the right
nail on the head thus :—

" The wish is, we verily believe, to obtain larger lumps of
the tempting cake of the educational grant, and hence the cry.
Already, school for school, the missionaries obtain much larger
grants than the natives, and if the Government Colleges could be
knocked on the head, there would be more money available for
Missionary Colleges. Those Colleges have been established
expressly for the suppression of the dearly loved religion of the
people, and the plan is to make the people pay, through the
Government, the cost of the engines that have been set up for
its overthrow. The Government cannot openly sanction grants
for the support of Christian Missions, but under the guise of
grants-in-aid to schools the matter may be easily and conveni-
ently managed. The missionaries know this well, and they
have set up their good-natured, religiously-disposed friends in
England and Scotland to lend their names to this movement,
which is purely missionary, and designed solely for the advancement of Missionary schools at Government cost. The "Council" is the mask, and the missionaries, as represented by Exeter
Hall, are its wearers. We cannot, we must frankly confess,
accord our sympathy to this unholy agitation."

Mr. Johnston and his fellow " Councillors" claim to
be animated by purely philanthropic motives. The

2

following passage occurs in the Reverend gentleman's reply to the Maharajah of Travancore, explaining the aims and objects of the "Council":—"Surely there is no necessity for seeking for a hidden motive for men endowed with ordinary feelings of philanthropy desiring to spread the blessings of education among the millions of India." Let the reader read, mark, learn, and inwardly digest the following passages from the Rev. J. Johnston's " Our Educational Policy in India" (the italics are ours). p. 8 :—

"With his (the Hindu's) primitive notions, he would have preferred to be ruled by a people whose God had given them power to subdue them, and if the Government exercised in his name, had been from the first wise and tolerant and just, we would have gained his obedience and respect, if not his affection and confidence. But this, I fear, is not now a practical question. It is vain to hope for any radical and beneficial change in *present circumstances.* It would now excite a not unreasonable suspicion to introduce a change, without *some adequate and obvious grounds* for an alteration of policy. *Circumstances may arise to justify such a step,* but as I cannot see how they can arise, *except through another revolt, or some justification of a great display of our power, and a call for a fresh proclamation of our authority,* I dare neither desire nor advocate such a change. I could not avoid asserting the principle, both because it is sound in policy, and because of its bearing on the question of education."

"There is a great leavening process going on in Hindu thought and feeling. There is a conviction diffused that the Christian system is the true, and will be the triumphant religion in India. *There will be opposition, there may be a conflict, imperiling our rule, if not our existence, in the country, ere that triumph is attained, but it will come,* and it will, we believe, come with a sudden and mighty rush which will startle and amaze an incredulous age." p. 54.

These passages, of course, read together, mean nothing more than that it would be a capital thing to have another Indian mutiny that Christianity might be propagated by the edge of the sword. But, may we ask, is this philanthropy?

III. The Missionaries claim that, while advocating the withdrawal of Government from the educational field they are the champions of all aided and independent education, whether missionary or other, but these claims are repudiated by the whole native community of Southern India.

The Rev. W. Miller, in the course of his examination of Mr. V. Krishnamachariar, a Trustee of Pacheappa's Charities, who appeared as a witness before the Education Commission at Madras, put the following question, and received the following reply :—

"Q. 18. May I ask whether you are aware that in all their repeated appeals against the policy of the late Director, the Council of the Christian College regarded themselves as fighting the battle of all aided education, that of Pacheappa's College no less than of their own ; and that next to securing fair play for their own institution nothing will give them so much pleasure as to help in securing the most liberal legitimate aid for all native effort, and most of all for Pacheappa's College as its most distinguished and most honourable example ?"

"A. 18. I am *not* aware of it."

On the other side we have the following evidence :—

(*a.*) The subjoined passage occurs in the evidence (p. 3) given before the Education Commission at Madras by the Honourable Mr. Justice T. Muttusami Iyer, c. i. e., of the High Court, Madras :— "As to the proposition that Higher Education may be transferred to private agencies, these must be either indigenous or missionary agencies, as to the former they have not yet come into existence, and as to the latter, they have no legitimate place in a scheme of national education ; and further, they carry no guarantee of permanency."

(*b.*) We will next quote in regard to this point a passage from the address presented to Dr. Hunter by the Trustees of Pacheappa's Charities, p. 2 :—

"We last year applied for an increased grant in strict conformity with the rules now in force, and while our application has met with no consideration, an additional grant of more than double the amount of the whole grant received by Patcheappa's High School has been recently given to a neighbouring institution conducted by foreign missionaries. Whatever may be the justification of such treatment, we venture to urge that a system of national education high or low, cannot be, and ought not to be made dependent on foreign missionary effort, and supported by the chance liberality of foreigners, and much less ought it to be dependent on, or connected with, the propagation of a foreign religion."

(c.) That influential body of native gentlemen, known as The Madras Native Association, say in para 2 of their address to Dr. Hunter :—

" As we believe that the Educational Department in this Presidency has been unjustly charged by some of the conductors and supporters of Mission institutions with having shown undue preference to Government institutions as against aided institutions in violation of the policy laid down in the Despatch of 1854, we desire to bear emphatic testimony to the fact that it has never been the aim of the Department to supersede or suppress private agencies that deserved to be helped and encouraged, and that its action has been mainly on the lines laid down in the Despatch. It seems to us that the assailants of the Educational Department assume that the intention of the Despatch was that a number of Government institutions should once for all be established and that thenceforward the efforts of the department should be directed towards reduction of State expenditure on them by converting them into aided institutions, and they point to the increase of expenditure on Government institutions as conclusive proof of their position."

(d) Mr. Krishnamachariar says at page 10 of his evidence:—

" Notwithstanding the reiterated assertion of the Missionaries that it is not their aim and wish to replace Government institutions by their own, but to have them handed over to the management of Boards of Hindu gentlemen, yet their uniform practice has been to have all such institutions transferred to their own management. As a matter of fact there are hardly any stable organized bodies of native growth such as are contemplated by the Despatch, and there cannot be for a long time to come ; but even if there were, the whole previous policy of the Missionaries shows that they would still continue to accept and press for the possession of a monopoly of education in the land, pleading that they are private " local " agencies.

IV. It is asserted by the Missionaries that the education given in Government Institutions is irreligious or godless in its character, and that it produces hostility to all religion ; but this is emphatically denied and proved to be false by less prejudiced observers.

(*a*) The Rev. W. Stevenson, Secretary, Free Church of Scotland Mission, Madras, says at p. 19 of his evidence :—

" Religious faith is a matter of free conviction, and when a Government recognises this, acknowledges religious faith as beyond the sphere of its control and leaves the various religions to their own truth and vitality, then it acts upon the true principle of religious neutrality. But if it ignores the very existence of religion and occupies a sphere in which religion should naturally find a place, but is excluded from it, then Government takes up a position practically antagonistic to all religion, and violates the most fundamental principle of religious neutrality. This is the position which the Government of India at present occupies in the sphere of education, and which it must continue to occupy so long as it is a direct educator. In order to be impartial towards all religions, it teaches none ; but in teaching no religion while yet it teaches other subjects, it proves itself practically hostile to all religion. This is not a matter of theory, but of actual experience. The influence of Government colleges and schools is felt by the earnest part of the native community to be anti-religious, and as being so, to be fraught with serious danger to the best interest of the social body."

(*b*) The Rev. J. Johnston says at p. 15 of his introduction to the second edition of "Our Educational Policy in India" :—

" When I call attention to the fact, that education in Government Colleges leads to irreligion, discontent, and disloyalty, let it be distinctly understood that I neither lay the entire blame on Government Colleges for the effects produced nor do I exempt other colleges from producing, in many cases, like results."

(*a*) On the other side we have the following valuable testimony of the Hon'ble Mr. Justice West of Bombay :—

" It is a matter of common observation that the generality of people placed in a new country amongst new associations sink in a marked degree in morality. The result occurs least amongst the most cultivated as these are the most nearly of one brotherhood everywhere, while the very manners of the uncultivated man show at once how incapable he is of self-government when released from the artificial bond of custom. Now in India propagandist teaching, even secular teaching, in a propagandist spirit, for which in itself I have no hard word or thought, produces in no small degree the same effect as emigration to another country. The old beliefs are shaken and shattered, the new ones do not take their place. The whole mass of moral and religious associations interwoven with the abandoned creed becomes discredited ; all propositions seem open to doubt ; the social tie of family affection and neighbouring kindness is loosened if not broken. There needs a refounding of the broken idol, but the glow of a deep conviction is wanting. The young man's principles moulded by tradition into a kind of organism have become mere fragments ; his life becomes fragmentary too, without definite purpose, without any pervading and harmonizing influence. All is hesitation, limpness, and half-resolves until the moral being, unless saved by the occupations and rough philosophy of active life, settles down into some form of feeble selfishness, or querulous dissatisfaction with things in general.

" Thus where the heathen youth is invited perseveringly to Christianity and fails to attain it, he is very apt to " fall between two moralities" with a complete indifference as to either. It is hard to suppose he can in any case benefit by this. In most cases he must suffer greatly if such be the end of his teaching. It is inevitable that religious teachers should make dogma the very corner-stone of the moral edifice ; they can find the appropriate sanction for anything that is good and beautiful in human conduct only in revelation, as thence too they draw their terrors for the evil-doer. When the premises are accepted all this is constraining and logical ; when they are not, it is simply ideal, or it is worse, by inducing a mock attention and solemnity while the heart and conscience are in no way moved. In such cases, the character must be moulded by examples which are accepted as real, by reasoning from premises known to be true, and appeals to those emotions which a man has as a man, not as the adherent of a creed. The dissoluteness which ensues on a disordered confluence of creeds and customs has been noticed and deplored by historians and philosophers from Plato to Lecky. Failing some sudden rapture of conversion, it is the secular teacher alone, who armed with a science unknown to earlier times, can prevent the inevitable revolution from being morally destructive. It is his function to show how on simply natural principles the present is the necessary outgrowth of the past ; that the old morality was the parent of the new ; that time which innovates greatly but gently links us alike to the past and the future is a ceaseless process of evolution. Here there is no violent disruption, no breaking down of the old structure, but rather a union of it with the new ; a feeling of the organic continuity of human existence is produced which leads to tranquillity, and shuts out contempt by intense personal interest in the whole history of the race. Definite instruction in duty must rest on this foundation, or on an admitted dogmatic foundation, to have any influence at all. The dogmatic foundation is not one on which a Government school can build, nor are mere principles of moral conduct learned by heart of any great efficacy in producing good behaviour. Morality in the abstract is about as effective as grammar in the abstract. The human disposition is social and imitative, benevolent and reverential. It is by enlisting these springs of conduct on the side of virtue that a living and working morality is produced, and they are to be won only by the presentation in some form of human action or suffering piercing straight to human wonder or tenderness. The plastic teacher is he who brings humanity in its noble aspects home to the consciousness of his pupils, who lives in the thoughts that he proclaims and gains disciples by his sincerity and the confidence which calls for confidence. I put this free philosophical teaching of course at what I conceive to be its best; but taking it so, it seems to be as far more influential than the other as freedom is superior to restraint. It can be accepted without misgiving; it can be applied without fear. But the Government cannot be indifferent to all that is so deeply moving the nature of its subjects. The thoughts of this generation determine the action of the next. British rule is committed to the task in India of fusing a civilization, the latest growth of time with the oldest still remaining. One means of effecting a great and abiding change would have been by a bold introduction of English institutions as capable of creating the popular force by which they would afterwards be supported. Another means would have been by asserting a complete predominance of English force. We have shrunk from that odious responsibility, but having done so, we, that is the Government, must brace itself to the task which a noble policy has entailed. It must endeavour to make itself felt through the whole scheme of the nation's development in such wise that this may be always advancing yet without abnormal growths and without estrangement from existing institutions. Of all men, therefore, those who govern in India will be the most short-sighted if they leave the great moving forces of the future to the impulse of mere chance. They must guide the movement through the education of the people and they must fit themselves to guide it aright on a secular basis."

(*b.*) The Honorable Mr. Justice Muttusami Iyer of Madras says in his evidence, in answer to the question, " Does definite instruction in duty and the principles of moral conduct occupy a place in the course of Government Colleges and Schools ? Have you any suggestions to make on this subject ?—

"No. I may, however, add that a strong sense of duty and a higher tone of moral conduct have practically resulted from the secular instruction afforded in Government Colleges and Schools. This is the testimony uniformly borne by men who have a practical knowledge of the country as it was 40 years ago and as it is at present."

(c.) Professor Lethbridge at p. 81 of his very able book on " High Education in India" writes :—

" And with regard to the moral teaching that is conveyed in Government Colleges, I will venture to quote some remarks that appeared in the *Hindoo Patriot*, of March 24, 1873, on a letter addressed by me, in that year, to the *Friend of India* on the subject :—

" Professor Lethbridge has addressed an excellent letter to the *Friend of India* on the subject of moral teaching in Government Colleges. He writes :—

" That the education imparted by our College lecturer is a godless one, or devoid of moral teaching, I distinctly and emphatically deny. It is true that we do not inculcate the doctrines of Christianity; even if the orders of Government did not forbid it, I very much doubt whether our duty as Christians and as men of honor would not preclude our doing so, paid as we are from the taxation of Hindoos and Mussulmans. But I unhesitatingly assert that the spirit of religion and morality, that spirit which not unknown under other systems and other faiths, has attained its highest purity and refinement in the teaching of Christ—is not absent from our lectures; indeed I am at a loss to know how such a subject as History can be adequately and sufficiently taught by a really conscientious and earnest lecturer without some infusion of that spirit. The *Friend* cannot gainsay this fact, but takes refuge under the flimsy excuse that the Government system of Education ' professedly and systematically ignores the religious emotions.' But, how can the Government introduce dogmatic religion—for the essence of all religions, fear of God and love of man, is as much inculcated in the Government schools as in any professedly religious schools—without breaking its faith with the people for religious neutrality. The *Friend* wishes to throw the whole work of national education into the hands of missionaries, but he may rest assured that our Government is too conscientious to do anything of the kind."

(*d.*) Dr. Duncan, of the Madras Presidency College, makes the following remarks, on the subject in the course of his thoughtful and valuable paper laid before the Education Commission :—

" The position of moral instruction in a scheme of education is one of those vexed questions which press for answer, but in regard to which there is great want of unanimity among educationists. In this, as in the case of many other practical questions, differences of opinion with respect to the means by which the end is to be attained are very frequently interpreted as difference of opinon with regard to the desirability of the end itself. But it may safely be affirmed that there is one and only one opinion among educationists as to the desirability of the end ; the education which cultivates the intellect, while leaving the moral nature a barren waste, being admitted on all hands to be only half culture.

" It is solely on the point of what is the best method to pursue in training the moral nature that divergencies arise among those engaged or interested in the education of the young. There are those who advocate definite and systematic teaching of the principles of morality as a branch of knowledge in the same way as other branches of the school curriculum are dealt with. I have some difficulty in forming a clear notion of what is really meant by this proposal. But if I understand it aright, I see endless difficulties in carrying it out, and even were these surmounted, I doubt whether the result would be as successful as its advocates anticipate. If morality is to be definitely and systematically taught like any other branch of knowledge, the teachers must themselves be definitely and systematically trained in the knowledge and application of moral principles ; if they are not so trained and their teaching is to depend on the moral knowledge which every fairly educated man is supposed to possess, that is tantamount to saying that the moral teaching is not, and need not be, systematic.

" A suitable text-book is also a desideratum if morality is to take a co-ordinate place with other branches of knowledge in a school curriculum. Suggestions have been made in various quarters as to the preparation of such a moral text-book. I am afraid that those who have set such a task before them will not find it a light one. The proposal to prepare a systematic text book of morality, so simple as to be intelligible to the capacities of school-going youth, and so catholic as to commend itself to the minds of all connected with education, appears to me Utopian. But the form which such a book would probably take would be that of a sort of moral anthology, in which moral examples culled from all available sources would be brought together so as to form a Moral Reader. Such a book would doubtless be very valuable and interesting in its way, but I am afraid it would not produce a homogeneous impression on the youthful mind. This moral kaleidoscope would be apt to leave in the mind a shifting phantasmagoria of virtues and vices, of duties and obligations, which would be of small service in the affairs of life.

" We must also be prepared to face another consequence of the introduction of a moral text-book whether in the form of a systematic treatise or in that of a moral anthology. No sooner will morality have been taken up definitely and systematically as a constituent part of our school curriculum, than a place will have to be made for it in our scheme of examination. Now if the examination be on the theory of morality merely, the end for which definite and systematic instruction in morality is sought will not be obtained. For a theoretical knowledge of ethics has neither less nor more value than theoretical knowledge of any other kind. If the examination be on practical morality, a genius will have to arise to teach us how moral character is to be valued by percentages of marks without the life and soul of it vanishing completely. It is difficult enough to estimate the growth of intellectual acquirements by written examinations, to value moral acquirements by the same means is impossible. It has long been a truism among educationists that when the best has been said in favour of public examinations, it must still be admitted that they fail completely to touch those subtler effects of school life—the development of the moral and spiritual elements of character. Of this, however, we may rest assured, that if moral training becomes a definite and distinct portion of the school curriculum, a demand will arise to subject it to the ordeal of a public, it may be of a competitive, examination.

" The advocates of a definite and systematic treatment of morality being made a distinct part of the school curriculum seem to forget how the moral character of the young is developed. Moral character is the confirmed habit of moral action, and its growth in the young of a school-going age is quite consistent with ignorance of the principles on which moral action proceeds. Moreover, the introduction of a young man, towards the close of his University career, to the study of the theory of ethics is often accompanied by effects the very opposite of what are anticipated. Principles which from his earliest years he has been uniformly taught to obey and which consequently have come to be a second nature, he now for the first time, in his life, sees subjected to the same rigid scrutiny as any of the laws of the material world. Rules of conduct which he has always regarded as self-evident, necessary and universal he now sees canvassed, questioned, it may be in the end rejected. This new experience has for a time anything but a steadying effect. Some come out of the ordeal like gold tried in the fire; others attain to the certainty of moral conviction only after a period of anxious doubt; while others, less fortunate, never recover their early faith in the sacredness of duty.

" I am firmly convinced that the attempt to teach morality like any other branch of knowledge as a part of a school curriculum will not prove successful in the way which its advocates anticipate. I would recommend that morality be taught in school in the way in which it is taught at home and in the social life of the young. In the life of every child and young person there are ample opportunities of inculcating all the fundamental duties as they actually arise in daily life. This is not the place to enumerate the various means adopted by parents and guardians to form and foster the character of those committed to their care. Suffice it to say that, along with precept and example harmoniously combined, there go active checking of wayward tendencies as they actually arise and willing assistance rendered in helping to overcome the difficulties that at first beset the path of duty. It is to the daily actual exercise of the virtues, to the actual performance of concrete duties, that we look, and must look, as the chief means of forming moral character. To this daily practice in duty, example, precept and theoretical knowledge are only auxiliaries.

" It is, therefore, to the actual exercise of the virtues and the actual performance of duties, that I would look for the formation of moral habits. And I maintain that this can be done as efficiently by means of any ordinary school curriculum as it could be after the introduction of the systematic teaching of morality as part of the school course, with the addition of moral text-books and moral competitive examinations. The teacher who cannot, within the ordinary school life, find the means and the opportunity of developing the moral character of his pupils, may rest assured that he has mistaken his profession.

" An opinion is abroad that facilities for moral training exist in aided, and especially in mission schools, which do not exist in Government schools—that in fact the cultivation of the moral nature is and must be excluded from the latter, and remains the peculiar monopoly of the former. To the epithet " godless," so freely and indiscriminately applied to Government institutions, many people add as a necessary corollary the epithet " immoral." But, in my answer to Question 60, I have endeavoured to shew that the really vital part of religion is no more excluded from Government schools and colleges than from those managed by the different theological sects. Whether or not the religious nature of the young be properly unfolded in Government establishments depends principally on the qualifications of the teachers ; and who will deny that the same is not the case in mission schools ? Consequently it may, and I believe often does, happen that pure and undefiled religion is in a healthier condition in the former than in the latter.

" But what I am here concerned with is not to adjust the comparative merits of the two classes of schools, but to defend Government schools and colleges against a charge bred of ignorant prejudice and fostered by sectarian animosity. And if on this subject I speak strongly it is because I feel strongly. To try to gloss over a matter of such moment with soft plausibilities and smoothly turned phrases would be to neglect a plain duty I owe to the Government which I serve, and to the people of this country whose welfare I am paid to promote. Now I cannot conceive it to be for the best interests of the people of India that they should be dragged into that mêlée of theological asperities and religious animosities characteristic of European ecclesiasticism ; and that too at a time when theological dogmatism and sectarian bitterness are gradually dying out in the West. To casual observers it may appear as if no such danger threatened India ; but any one who looks below the surface must see that the different sects of missionaries, with one or two remarkable exceptions, while seemingly united in their opposition to a so-called system of secular education, are secretly consumed with mutual jealousies, which require only the abolition of Government schools and colleges to burst into flame.

" The allegations that Government institutions are forbidden to cultivate the religious nature of the young, and that, as a consequence, they cannot and do not develop the moral nature, I look upon as misleading and mischievous. To shew that the latter allegation is untrue I have to appeal to the *Standing Orders* of the Educational Department of this Presidency, which are binding on almost all Government schools. In the *Standing Orders* moral training is distinctly laid down as a matter demanding the earnest attention of the teacher. Now, putting aside the supposition that this subject has been introduced by the Director merely for the purpose of making a show of virtue which the Government system does not and cannot possess, there remain two alternative hypotheses : either that the teachers wilfully treat this provision of the *Standing Orders* as a dead letter, or that there are difficulties in the way of carrying it out in a Government school which do not exist in a mission or aided school. The former alternative, though not unfrequently thrust in a sneering way in the face of the officers of the Department, does not deserve a moment's serious consideration. The latter alternative, being the one adopted by many highly estimable people, Native as well as European, is worthy of careful enquiry. The obstacle which is supposed to stand in the way of moral training in Government schools is the absence of religious teaching. That the educational officers of the State should be debarred from teaching religion appears a sufficiently bad state of affairs ; but that they should, as a consequence, be prevented from inculcating the truths of morality, if not worse, in the abstract, appears to be more dangerous on account of the important practical consequences. For, this latter disability, if it did exist, would imperil the whole fabric of society ; and in that light it is viewed with grave anxiety by many thoughtful Natives of this country, Hindus and Muhammadans alike. To relieve such anxiety I repeat , firstly, that the aspect of religion which bears upon morality is no more excluded from Government schools and colleges than from any other ; and secondly, even if religion were excluded, opportunity and scope would still remain for the teacher to develop the moral character of his pupils. Nobody worth listening to will now-a-days contend that the fundamental principles of ethics rest on the theological dogmas peculiar to any particular sect. The best moralists of all ages and creeds have held that morality does not rest on any dogmatic theological basis whatever. So that, in being debarred from inculcating any theological creed, Government educational officers are merely prevented from teaching something which is not essential to morality. It is the emotional element in religion which comes into close relation with moral action. A virtuous life implies an habitual impulse or motive to do right and abstain from wrong. This impulse or motive is made up of feelings of various kinds. In fact there is no emotion of the human breast which may not become a minister of good. Here we have the true answer to the question—in what relation does morality stand to religion. Religion (meaning by that term, not the body of theological beliefs, but the aggregate of feelings called up when we contemplate the Deity and our relation to him) is one of the most powerful among the diverse motives of human conduct. And as I have endeavoured to show, there is nothing in the constitution of Government colleges and schools to hinder the teacher from fostering the growth of genuine religious feeling in his pupils, and nothing, therefore, to prevent his appealing to those religious feelings as one of the sanctions of moral conduct. Whether this be done or not depends, as I have said, on the personal character of the teacher: and this is as true of mission institutions as of Government schools. Nor must it be forgotten how large a part of morality is concerned with the relations of man to his fellowmen. I have spoken of the religious feelings as constituting only *one* of the sanctions of morality; for we must not ignore the efficacy of other feelings as motives to right conduct. Among those other feelings are to be reckoned those which regard self and those which regard our fellowmen. So that, even were he precluded from appealing to the religious feelings of the young, the teacher in a Government institution would still have the wide field of personal and social interests to work in; and who will say that to work this field thoroughly and well is not arduous enough to tax the energies of the best of men, and efficacious enough to train up a nation of wise and good citizens? Fortunately, however, Government educational officers have the same commission as others, namely, to train the moral nature by appealing to every feeling of the human heart, to the religious feelings no less than to the personal and social. To prove that they have not been altogether unsuccessful in the performance of their task, I appeal to the most convincing of evidence —to the stainless and upright lives of the many men all over India who have been trained in Government institutions, and who, as respects moral character, need not fear comparison with the educated classes of any country."

(*e.*) Dr. W. H. Wilson, Professor of Physical Science, Presidency College, Madras, says at p. 6 of his evidence :—

"There is not an intelligent and unprejudiced native in this Presidency who does not scout the pretensions to the possession of a monoply of moral teaching which certain missionaries lose no opportunity to urge, especially in distant lands and before sympathetic audiences where there is little fear of contradiction, who does not deride the notion of Missionary Colleges producing men in any way better or more moral than those trained in Government institutions. If there be any difference in this respect, the superiority will I imagine be generally conceded to the men whose education was received in the " godless" colleges ; those colleges whose existence we have been told is a peril to the country, and which are training up a race of Atheists such as the world never saw. In purity of life, in rectitude of conduct, and in conscientious discharge of their public or professional duties, the men thus calumniated, are admitted to be excelled by none, certainly not by those for whom so vast a superiority is claimed. Much sympathy has been enlisted for Missionary enterprise, and much hostility towards Government education created, by accusations of this nature, and though easily refuted in this country, it is more difficult to meet them when made in Europe. Indeed it is impossible to counteract the evil effect they produce, as these charges, through persistent reiteration, obtain a much wider circulation than their denial ever does."

(*f*) H. H. The Maharajah of Travancore, a thoughtful and worthy representative of native ideas, says at page 7 of his "Letter to Mr. Grant Duff" :—

"I do not comprehend the truth of the remark that the education at present given in Government schools and colleges has reared a race of atheists. Surely it has been powerfully instrumental in sweeping away the dross and scum of every religion. But it *has not* extinguished, *it cannot* extinguish, that instinctive desire which exists in every human being to know the unknowable and to define the infinite. The most out-and-out atheist, who prides himself in his atheism and drags atheism to his aid, must have at times felt in his inner man the sore need of invoking a Superior Power and a Superior Dispensation. Good and sound secular education can never harm this religious instinct; but, on the other hand, it makes a man better fitted to think correctly and to seek the truth diligently. There is no dearth of religious teaching in India. It can be had for the asking, and often without the asking. I can with confidence affirm that there is an honest yearning in the minds of most educated natives after a religion. They have all the materials before them, and they may be left to make their choice."

(*g.*) Mr. Lethbridge in his " High Education in India," (p. 124) says :—

" At present, in the many famous Missionary Colleges of India, the teaching is most efficient in the highest branches of Mathematics, of Philosophy, of Natural Science, of the whole " profane" learning of the Universities ; but in the matter of religion, General Tremenhere has shown that a little perfunctory Bible reading for perhaps an hour or less each day is all that is ventured on—and it has been stated that the proved conversion of one of the students would probably have the effect of emptying the College to which he belonged."

V. The Missionaries and the " Council " wish the Government to withdraw from the direct management of education in order that the power and importance of the Missionary Colleges and Schools may be augmented largely and at once, and that wider opportunities may be afforded the Missionary Societies for uprooting the religious beliefs of the people of India and converting them to Christianity, (*a*). The Revd. J. Johnston in " Our Educational Policy in India'' (Introduction p. iv.) says :—

" Christian educationists saw that if the provisions for aiding equally Native and Mission Schools and Colleges, as was most explicitly promised and provided for in the Despatch, were faithfully carried out there would be no difficulty in the way of the rapid and almost indefinite extension of Christian instruction ; not by asking any special favor for their institutions over those of the natives ; not by any forcing of Christianity by Government authority ; but by the natural and laudable method of providing the highest form of education in secular studies, along with the knowledge of Divine truth and the love of God, which commend themselves to the understanding and heart even of the heathen when taught in a loving and sympathetic spirit.''

Again (Introduction p. 15.)

" A weak objection is made to the proposal to withdraw the colleges supported by Government, on the ground, that if the Natives came forward in any force to supply their place, the effect would be the same, as the higher education necessarily overturns their heathen systems, based as they are on physical errors.

" But surely there is a vast difference between undermining the religious beliefs of the heathen by Government Officials, in Government Colleges, paid out of Government taxes derived from a heathen population, and the heathen upsetting their own creed, in their own colleges, by teachers of their own choice."

In the same pamphlet at p. 53 occurs the following :—

" Another point of great importance is to see that such a staff of Professors and Teachers is kept up, as shall admit of greater attention being paid to Evangelistic work in the colleges and amongst those who have passed through our educational institutions.''

(*b*) The Rev. Dr. G. U. Pope, in a paper on " India as a Field for Christian Missions,'' read at the York Missionary Conference in July last, gives a fuller and more forcible exposition of the Missionary views and aims in this matter, thus :—

" But what I desire especially to urge upon you at this time is *the opening now afforded for the Propagation of Christianity in India by means of Christian schools and colleges.* A volume might be written upon the subject. How superficially it must be treated in a twenty minutes' paper! You know how ably this work was inaugurated by Dr. Alexander Duff of Calcutta, followed in Bombay by Dr. John Wilson, and in Madras by Mr. Anderson ; carried on ever since by men hardly inferior to these pioneers ; and now, especially in Madras, conducted in the " Christian College" under Mr. William Miller ;* in Masulipatam by worthy successors of Noble and Fox ; and in various schools and colleges maintained by the Venerable Society for the Propagation of the Gospel in Foreign Parts aided by her Venerable Sister, the Society for the Promotion of Christian Knowledge, by the Church Missionary Society, ever ready to engage in any good work, by the Scottish Presbyterian Boards of Missions, which send out generally men of distinguished ability, by various congregations of Jesuit Fathers, in Calcutta, Bombay, Negapatam, and elsewhere, by the Wesleyan Missionary Society, by the London Missionary Society, and by others whose work is in various degrees valuable.

" This work so variously carried on (with many defects and anomalies, with much waste of power from lack of oneness) I regard as by far the most hopeful and far-reaching of all our missionary operations, and I desire to see the day when all the centres of Hindu life shall have Christian schools of every grade and colleges established in their midst.

" These institutions are commended to us by the fact that they are largely self-supporting after a time ; since Native students are generally able and willing to pay adequate fees where the English teaching is first rate, while the Government is ready to give liberal grants-in-aid, without in the least degree interfering with the liberty of the teachers to inculcate Christian truth.

" To return : the masters, if men of ability and especially if of University distinction, are constantly appointed examiners in the various Indian Universities ; and are among the most influential Fellows of those universities ; and are really great powers in the places where they labour : *Christ powers in a heathen land.*

" It is, however, very desirable that they should be men of mark, so as to give a *status* to our Christian Colleges.

" The curious mistake has been not unfrequently made of sending to such work trained schoolmasters, not animated by any Missionary spirit ; and even of relegating to this all-important work men who, for any cause, were not considered eligible candidates for Holy Orders. Thus, we have had, and we now have, many moderately successful schools without any appreciable or distinct Missionary effectiveness : large salt heaps without savour. Many have found themselves sitting in Duff's seat,

* The High Churchman, it may be remarked, refuses the title of *reverened* to the presbyterian parson.

with but a very moderate portion of his remarkable ability, and still less of his burning and apostolic zeal. With such (nominally) Mission Schools I have scant sympathy, and I look upon them with but the faintest hope of benefit in a Missionary point of view.

"A reform is needed, especially in the schools of our own Church of England Missions.

"Every such institution, I submit, should have at least two able and zealous Missionaries at its head, one as principal of the department, and one devoting himself to direct Missionary work among the educated English-speaking society that gathers around it.

"Through these, others may be reached. Such Missionaries need not, at first, much trouble themselves to learn native languages, as their first and best work is in English.

"If in the vicinity of every such institution not less than two like-minded *zenana* sisters were engaged in striving to create a Christian influence in the homes of the students, to which they would have easy access, the two works combined would have a fourfold effect; then boys would be taught in college, and their sisters would be influenced at home, and they would compare notes.

"At this time the Government of India is seeking to withdraw itself in great measure from the higher education of the country; and, as India will have English education, this is a great missionary opportunity.

"Only let me repeat, second-rate men must not be sent out for this work. It requires the best men. It is full of interest and promise for them; it is quite worthy of them. The institution will soon become self-supporting; and the salaries given (though a missionary must not go out for his salary) should be such as to place them beyond all sordid anxieties, beyond all necessity of seeking for other emoluments to bring up their families respectably in the station of life to which they themselves belong.

"Having regard to the specialities of our Indian social life it is not expedient that our missionaries should be very poor men. Health is sacrificed, powers of body and mind enfeebled, life often endangered by unsuitable and unnecessary deprivations in such a climate, and in a work where the *mens sana in corpore sano* is so necessary."

The meaning of the above, in plain English, is that now is the opportunity for Missionary Societies to step in and found colleges, and that Missionary Professors should be paid handsome salaries. Is not this worldly object then really at the bottom of a good deal of this agitation for the disestablishment of State Colleges?

Dr. Pope concludes this significant address on India as a Field of Missions and *Christian* education as their real strength, in unmistakable words thus :—

"Let it be granted that immediate conversions even of the lowest, and even where the motives are mixed, are cause of real thankfulness ; yet, I ask your sympathy on behalf of a work of ampler scope, which is, in truth, placing a mighty lever under the very foundations of Hinduism, and must over-turn it in the end."

VI. The Missionaries and the "Council" say that the great aim of their agitation is " to secure the faithful and vigorous carrying out of the great princi-ples of the Despatch of 1854," (Reply to the Letter of H. H. the Maharajah of Travancore, p. 7); but that Despatch is not framed with the intention of aiding proselytism ; and if that would be the inevi-table result of carrying out what the Missionaries contend are its provisions, then every Government would be compelled to say that those provisions must not be carried out.

Now, why do Missionaries want Government to withdraw from education ? This is a very simple question, and the following quotations from the Rev. J. Johnston, the exponent of the views of the party advocating withdrawal, will to most peo-ple furnish a sufficient answer :—

"Another point of great importance is to see that such a staff of professors and teachers is kept up, as shall admit of greater attention being paid to evangelistic work in the col-leges and amongst those who have passed through our educa-tional institutions.

"This work must, as a rule, be done by the professors, not by a separate class set apart as evangelists. They would be looked on with distrust, and would not get the hold on old scholars which a former teacher would. Every professor and teacher must be an evangelist, who carries his evangelistic spirit into the school and college, every day, and at all times. By having a larger staff, there could always be one in turn engaged in looking after, and addressing as occasion offered, old graduates of their own or Government colleges in the towns and by occasional itinerancy in the surrounding country for scattering the seed of the word where it may fall into the hearts of old pupils and recall old lessons. (p. 53).

" When Hinduism falls, it will fall as those grand old towers fall which have outlived the age and state of society for which they were constructed ; so strongly cemented that they will stand or fall entire—they cannot be taken down like our frail modern structures, stone by stone. It is only by the slow and persevering process of sapping and mining that they can be brought to the ground, and they fall in one solid mass. It is thus that this great donjon, in which superstition and caste have kept the millions of India as in a castle of despair, will one day fall, "to rise no more at all." A thousand agencies are at work to undermine it, secular and religious, and we wish them all God-speed ; but none can compare with the full and clear proclamation of the glorious Gospel, in thoroughly equipped and efficiently conducted educational institutions, in which Divine light is thrown on every subject of human study, by generous and disinterested men of the highest culture and Christian character." (p. 55.)

The advocates of the abolition or transfer of State colleges habitually refer to para. 62 of the despatch as the authority they rely upon. The paragraph runs thus, and the particular attention of the reader is requested to the portions we have italicised :—

" We look forward to the time when any *general system of education* entirely provided by government may be discontinued with the gradual advance of the system of grants-in-aid, and when many of the existing government institutions, especially those of the higher order may be *safely* closed, or transferred to the management of *local* bodies under the control of, and aided by, the State. But it is far from our wish *to check the spread of education in the slightest degree by the abandonment of a single school to probable decay*; and we, therefore, entirely confide in your discretion, and in that of the different local authorities, while keeping this object steadily in view, *to act with caution*, and to be guided by *special* reference to the *peculiar circumstances* which affect the demand for education in different parts of India."

That the interpretation put on this paragraph of the Despatch of 1854 by the missionaries is a perverse one, is plain from the following extract from a subsequent explanatory despatch of Her Majesty's Secretary of State to the Government of

India, No. 6, of the 14th May 1862, which strangely enough has been kept in the back ground in the Missionary controversy all this time :—

" Her Majesty's Government are unwilling that a Government school should be given up in any place where the inhabitants show a marked desire that it should be maintained."

Is not this an authoritative interpretation of a much disputed paragraph, which though perfectly clear to all unprejudiced minds and past Governments, has been wilfully contorted for vain and selfish ends by those whose aim is to make capital out of the educational agitation in India? And has not Her Majesty's Government in this latter despatch pledged not only itself but the Government of India to an educational policy directly contrary to that of the Missionaries and the " Council ?"

This explanatory despatch of 1862 seems to us in the present state of matters to be a document of the first importance, and the only conclusion that can be drawn from it, and from the summary of the objects of the great Despatch given in para. 6 of the Resolution of the Government of India constituting the Education Commission, is that not only the maintenance of State colleges and schools of the higher order, but also the increase of their number when necessary, was contemplated ; and wherever the need was felt, and spontaneous local efforts could not be entirely depended upon for the establishment and efficient maintenance of private institutions, it was the obvious duty of the educational authorities to start and maintain on an efficient footing Government institutions out of the taxes paid by the native population, as an integral part of a complete scheme of national education for India.

If this conclusion is sound, then it is plain that it was a most unjust and uncharitable act of the Rev. J. Johnston and his " Council " in England, and of certain Missionaries in Madras, to misrepresent the action of Colonel Macdonald and other educational officers as an unauthorised deviation from the principles of the Despatch of 1854, and to attack them personally for having honestly stood firm to the distinctly defined policy of Her Majesty's Government, and deprecated the closing of Government schools and the replacing of them by foreign Mission schools according to the missionary scheme.

If any one is still in doubt as to the inaccuracy of the missionary interpretation of the educational Despatch of 1854, we think his doubts will be removed by a perusal of the following examination of the disputed paragraph in that despatch by Mr. Lethbridge, at page 42 of his work on " High Education in India" :—

"The Despatch further looks forward to the time ' when many of the existing Government institutions, especially those of the higher order, may be safely closed, or transferred to the management of local bodies under the control of and aided by the State.' Now, many people will be surprised to find that the sentence I have here quoted is the *only one* (except a cursory reference in Section 86) in the whole despatch that can, by any stress of interpretation, be held to give even a shadow of foundation for the theories of the abolitionists ; and a careful examination of the context will show (1) that no reference whatever is here made or intended to the State Colleges, and (2) that no other educational institution of any kind is to be abandoned or transferred, unless its place can be fully and adequately supplied. The authors of the Despatch distinctly say, in the very next sentence, ' it is far from our wish to check the spread of education in the slightest degree by the abandonment of a single school.' They say nothing whatever, in this connection, of the Colleges. I shall show, that the exact functions of the State Colleges cannot possibly be *fully and adequately* performed by institutions conducted or controlled in any other way."

VII. It is asserted by the Missionaries that, were Government to withdraw from taking a direct part in education, and carry out the Despatch of 1854, as interpreted in their own way, native agencies would at once supply its place in the educational field ; but we scout the idea in common with others who have an intimate acquaintance with the country, and its real wants and protest in the most emphatic manner, against the withdrawal of Government from education.

(*a*). The Revd. J. Johnston in the second edition of his " Our Educational Policy in India" says at p. 42 :—

" Both Mr. Kempson and Mr. Cust assume that in advocating the withdrawal of the Government Colleges we expect that the grants-in-aid are to go exclusively, or almost exclusively, to mission colleges, and against this their arguments on the ground of neutrality are telling enough. The Natives of India have a right to be fairly and even liberally dealt with in such a case; and I fully expect that they would set themselves to establish and maintain colleges and high schools, if they were left to stand alone, instead of being bolstered up by a pauperising system. They have done so before, and would do it again. When the desire for education had not a tithe of the strength it has now, the natives of India made noble contributions for education. Now it is a felt necessity, and there is no fear of the higher education going down. If the Universities are kept up, they will maintain the standard in all the higher schools and colleges."

(*b*) The following is from the Revd .W. Stevenson's evidence, p. 15 :—

" It follows from what I have said on the preceding question, that in my opinion the withdrawal of Government from the direct management of schools and colleges would have a most encouraging effect upon the spread of education.

" In the first place, it would be a convincing evidence that the Government really desired independent bodies to extend their operations, evidence which they are much in want of at present. Not only do missionary agencies feel that they are under the present system heavily handicapped and discouraged, but independent native gentlemen are deterred from opening schools which might be regarded as rivals to Government institutions. I have, for example, very good authority for stating that the College Department of Pacheappa's Institution would have been developed sooner and further than it is, had it not been that it would thereby appear to be a rival and possible substitute for the Presidency College.

" Further, were Government to withdraw from direct operations, it would have considerable funds set free to encourage aided institutions, and to call forth other resources which are not at present available. Every rupee of aid given by Government calls forth another, and in most cases two, from independent managers, not to speak of the fees contributed by the people themselves. A great extension of education could thus hardly fail to be the result.

" Thirdly such withdrawal would tend greatly in my opinion to promote a spirit of reliance upon local exertions and combination for local purposes," which the present system tends to repress. It cannot be expected that the people will step forward to do for themselves what Government is doing for them, especially when they think such spontaneous activity on their part would be the reverse of agreeable to Government authorities. It is certainly a main part of the educational influence of Government institutions to teach the people to look to Government for every thing—to expect from Government first education, then certificates, and then appointments; and to see no field for exertion or enterprise outside of the Government service. Government overshadows every thing in India, and the sense of its omnipresence and omnipotence fills the mind of almost every Educated native, so that there seems no scope, or career beyond it. The existence of a Government educational department is not entirely to blame for this, but undoubtedly it has much to do with it. In Government schools the youths are first inculcated with the idea, and early impressions are proverbially lasting. Were Government to withdraw from the direct management of Educational institutions, and hand them over to independent local bodies, a great blow would be given to the pernicious error—the mother of discontent and disloyalty, that Government is bound first to manufacture an educated class and then provide for it. Until this is done, it seems to me that the prospect of making local self-government a reality is very doubtful indeed. To transfer Government schools to independent local bodies would be the most effective step in this direction. Education is a field in which the spirit of reliance upon local exertions and combination for local purposes can be most safely and wisely developed. I have no doubt also that if a stimulus were once given to a spirit of loyal freedom and active enterprise, it would manifest itself in many directions, and in due time develope the resources and promote the prosperity and wealth of the country."—

But in reply to these statements, we will quote the following native opinions and evidence of gentlemen who know India well and sympathise with its people :—

(*a*) His Highness the Maharajah of Travancore in his published "Letter" to the Governor of Madras writes at p. 5 :—

" To argue therefore that the cause of higher education, which thrives in England independently of all State support, could be well left to private agencies in the case of India, is to argue from false analogy. The time may come when the chiefs and well-to-do men of India, themselves benefited by higher education, will contribute to it in such a manner as to relieve the Government of the obligation. That there is such a tendency is evident from the Colleges and High Schools that are springing up in Native States and the scholarships founded by native chiefs and native communities in Government Colleges. It is very necessary to encourage such a tendency ; and nothing can have a more disastrously opposite effect than the withdrawal, at the present stage, of Government connection with higher education, which is certain to be construed into a public duooemnation of it."

„ In answer to this it is, I believe, urged by the Christian Missionaries and their friends and supporters that if the Natives of India will not, in their own interests, maintain higher education, the Christian benevolence of England is ready to do it for them, and that with the additional advantage of giving at found religious tone to that education. I do not for a moment underestimate the valuable service which the earnest and self-denying labors of the Missionaries have done to the cause of education in India. Nor do I undervalue a greater religious leavening of education in India. In his excellent University address, every word of which will long be remembered, and in which the outpourings of an earnest and loving heart at times unconsciously overflow the limits of strict official bounds, the Viceroy, Lord Ripon, regrets the absence of the religious element in the present system of State education. In this regret all thoughtful men must cordially agree. At the same time, His Lordship most justly observes that a Government ruling over millions of alien people of diversified creeds cannot take any action to rectify this. To withdraw from the present system of directly supporting higher education and to entrust it to Missionary agencies is sure to be attributed, reasonably or otherwise, to a desire on the part of Government to force Christian teaching upon the people. The reluctance to be educated in Missionary Schools may be less manifested by Hindus than by Mahomedans, Parsis, Sikhs, &c., but all must share it to a very great extent. In this remark I refer to the higher classes especially."

(*b*) Mr. C. Runga Charlu, c. i. e., Dewan of Mysore, whose enlightened views and wide experience are well known, says in his speech at the Anniversary of the Maharajah's College, on the 24th March 1882 :—

" The questions which are being now discussed in connection with education are how far Government can be relieved of the cost of higher education and how the education of the masses at large can be extended. You may have seen that the enlightened ruler of Travancore, who has an extensive knowledge of educational matters, has already sounded the note of warning against the adoption of any suicidal policy in respect of higher education. There is a general feeling amongst natives, and I may add amongst those European gentlemen who have most laboured in the cause of education with a love for the people, that high-class education is not viewed in a proper light. The idea of placing higher education and the education of the masses in antagonism with each other has not, as you are aware, originated with the natives of this country. It has been put forward by a deputation in England, who are, it is believed, influenced by the missionary bodies here, who desire to take the management of higher education into their own hands. This, I need hardly say, is simply impossible in the circumstances of India, and it is to be regretted that by this move our missionary bodies, to whom the country owes so much in the matter of education, should have needlessly exposed themselves to the distrust and dissatisfaction of educated natives. But you will have seen that the resolution of the Government of India on the subject indicates a desire to make over the educational institutions only to native gentlemen, when they are prepared to take charge of them. *It would have been better if this idea was not put forward at all, as natives are not, and will not for a long time to come, be ready to take charge of high education,* and meanwhile the suggestion might unsettle the management of these institutions. Even if competent natives could be found, how could these really public schools be handed over to them any more than to missionary bodies, without giving rise to serious objections in other quarters ?"

(*c*) In his speech at the Convocation of the University of Madras, held on the 23rd March 1882, Mr. Justice Mutusami Iyer clearly set forth the views of the Hindu community when he said :—

" Doubtless the ultimate state of things to be aimed at in regard to higher education would be a model college in the Presidency town, supported by the State, forming as it were a focus of intellectual life, and having on its staff professors of eminence, who are in themselves the living embodiments of the highest forms of culture. No expense would be spared by the State to maintain the instruction imparted in such an institution at the level of attainable perfection. Such a college the ordinary laws of demand and supply cannot be trusted to bring into existence. In the provinces would then spring up colleges supported by the nobility and gentry and an enlightened middle class fully alive to the advantages of liberal education, and able and willing to make large sacrifices for securing it to their childern. These colleges would necessarily be influenced by the high standard maintained at the Government College, but not enslaved by it; they would provide for a variety of forms of culture, according to the importance attached to the several branches of knowledge or method of instruction in the communities among whom they come into existence. *Admitting that this should be the final aim, I must express my conviction that the day is yet distant when such a state of things may be expected in this country.* Those who have benefited by the encouragement accorded by the State to higher education *hither-to*, have not been the zemindars and the landed aristocracy of the country, so far at least as this Presidency is concerned, and there is no such sharp distinction between the rich and the poor in this *country*, as is said to exist in European countries, and intelligence and refinement do not co-exist with wealth to the extent that it does elsewhere. *It is to be feared, in the present circumstances, if the State aid be suddenly withdrawn, any movement to replace it out of the private wealth of the country would not be successful in most cases. Higher education will have to be practically left in the hands of missionary agencies, in no sense indigenous.* I do not in the least undervalue the important services which they have rendered to the cause of education. But if all higher education is virtually committed to their hands will it conduce to the variety of culture and the adaptation to the special needs of the country upon which so much stress is laid, in recommending the withdrawal of State support to higher education? However this may be, it would certainly seem anomalous that, in a country composed of many nationalities, Hindus, Mahomedans, Buddhists, we should trust for the provision for higher education which has such an important influence on national progress, not to indigenous agencies, which there is reason to fear will take time to come into existence, not to the private wealth of the country, a considerable proportion of which still remains to be brought under the influence of culture, but to the benefactions of charitable men in England and foreign countries, contributed for a special purpose, and to their willingness to permit such benefactions to be applied for the purpose of secular education. Apart from other objections, such a system will be without the guarantee of permanence and stability, which is essential to a scheme of national education.

[d] The Revd. N. Rondy, of Coimbatore, says in his evidence, p. 3 :—

" Is the time come for Government to give up its colleges and schools ?

" I beg to quote the words of a most influential native gentleman on the subject : ' It would have been better if this idea was not put forward at all for the suggestion might unsettle the management' of the already existing institutions.

" The present state of India is, it may be said, a transitional period. The Indian people begin to shake off the chains of routine and to throw away many of their prejudices. It appears that the time is come for Government, in order to reap the most precious fruits of the liberal education they have afforded to the natives, to exercise a proper control over this awakening of the Indian people. How will Government control it if not by education ? A native gentleman said lately that ' the Government colleges alone can command the advantages of bringing all classes of men, who are to be the leaders of the public thought, on an arena of common thought and mutual good will.

" In the Resolution of the Government of India it is said that by the withdrawal of Government from the direct management of colleges and schools ' the native community will be able to secure that freedom and variety of education, which is an essential condition in any sound and complete educational system.' Were the Indian people one, such policy would be certainly the most suitable for the promotion of education, but if we consider that it is composed of so many classes widely differing from each other by caste or creed, we may say that unity is impossible in such variety, and without such unity a sound and complete educational system seems impossible. It is not sufficient to foster the spirit of independence specially in the matter of education, it must be directed and controlled. The Government colleges alone can afford such control in the present state of India.

" It is then more necessary than ever for Government to retain all its institutions. If, at such a moment, the Government were to withdraw totally or even to a large extent from the direct management of colleges and schools it would certainly prove fatal not only to education but to Government itself.

" Since the question has been moved, the public opinion has been much offended. Such step is disapproved by the best educated native gentlemen. Such contemplated withdrawal is looked upon in every Indian quarter with distrust and disaffection.

" So the Catholic Bishops of Southern India, who are certainly in a position to judge of the pernicious effects which such a measure could possibly have on Government and education have not hesitated to warn the Government through the Education Commission against such a *faux pas*."

(*e*) The Hon'ble Mr. Justice West of Bombay says :—

" It (Government) must endeavour to make itself felt through the whole scheme of the nation's development in such wise that this may be always advancing yet without abnormal growths and without estrangement from existing institutions. Of all men, therefore, those who govern in India will be the most short-sighted if they leave the great moving forces of the future to the impulse of mere chance. They must guide the movement through the education of the people and they must fit themselves to guide it aright on a secular basis."

(*f*) Dr. D. Duncan says in his evidence what is in complete accord with the Hindu view :—

" There is every reason to believe that what has generally happened in the past would usually happen again, on the closure or transfer of a Government institution of the higher order. The ' private bodies' would in nine cases out of ten be the agents of some one of the missionary societies. Now I cannot conceive that it was the intention of the framers of the Despatch of 1854, or that it is the desire of the Government of India, to see education practically taken out of the hands of the natives of the soil and monopolized by persons acting under instructions from committees in great Britain or elsewhere. If Government really desires to foster self-help among the people (and I entertain as little doubt about that as I do about its being the duty of Government to cultivate it), more care should be taken than is usually done to see that the closure or transfer of the State school has that effect. As a rule the worst measure that could be adopted to secure that end is to hand it over to one of the missionary bodies. A missionary school is to a certain extent a charity school. Now if it were proposed to rouse a community to private effort in the management of its own affairs, it would hardly conduce to that end if a foreign society were to establish a soup kitchen, or a work-house, where food or shelter could be obtained at only a fraction of its value. This would be to pauperize the people rather than to stimulate self-help. And nothing but the glamour of false sentiment prevents people from seeing that a system of education largely supported by foreign charity must have the same pauperizing tendency. On the other hand, there are as yet very few districts in which the transfer of a Government institution of the higher order to the management of the local committees of native gentlemen would not act injuriously on education. The reasons for this will be found in my answer to Q. 36. With the spread of the higher education, every year will see it becoming more easy to make such a transfer with impunity." (p. 4.)

VIII. The missionaries assert that were the Government Colleges annihilated the standard of instruction would not deteriorate ; but this is not the opinion of those who know the country at least as well as the missionaries.

(a) The Revd. E. Sell, Secretary, C. M. S., Madras, says in his evidence in answer to question 38 as to the risk of a deterioration in the standard of instruction in the event of the withdrawal of Government from the direct management of schools or colleges :—

(a) " No, for the University fixes the standard, not the Government Colleges."

The Revd. W. Stevenson says, in answer to the same question :—

(b) "In the event of the Government withdrawing to a large extent from the direct management of schools or colleges I see no reason whatever to apprehend that the standard of instruction in any class of institutions would deteriorate. I do not see that at present Government institutions can claim the honor of maintaining the highest standard. It may be, that taking Government institutions as one class and all aided institutions as a second class, the former show better results at the University and other examinations than the latter. But such a mode of comparison is manifestly unfair. Government institutions may rightly enough be placed in one category, as they are all organized in the same way and are under the same management. But with aided institutions the case is very different. They are under all sorts of managing bodies and vary indefinitely in their equipment and efficiency. Some of them are but adventure schools of yesterday, while others are older than, as well as organized and manned and quite as efficient as any Government institutions. It is no just comparison therefore to throw them all into one class and set them over against the compact body of Government schools and thus find an easy demonstration th for superiority of direct Government to aided education. But let the best of the one class be compared with the best of the other and the aided institutions will, I submit, be quite equal to those of Government.

"Further if Government schools are transferred to local bodies I do not see why they should not continue as efficient as before. The University standards will not be lowered, the teaching staff is not likely to be smaller or less efficient and the Director and Inspectors will still remain to encourage and stimulate the managers."

The evidence of enlightened observers is however different. The following is the evidence of—

(a). The Hon'ble Mr. Justice West :—

" I conclude that the benevolence which sustains the Freen General Assembly's Institution and St. Xavier's College is by no means wasted, but these institutions would not take the place of the Government colleges, if only because the people could not use them. If the absence of competition did not make them more distinctly propagandist, they would, at any rate, be suspected of it ; this would keep many youths away, and in fact they would almost inevitably fall into a subordination of their secular teaching to the main ends of their being. The University could not keep their scholarship up to the mark when it had only their own professors to choose from for its examiners in the higher examinations."

(b). H. H. The Maharajah of Travancore (p. 7 of his " Letter to Mr. Grant Duff") writes :—

" It is further doubtful whether, when once entrusted to Missionary agencies, higher education will continue to retain its present high standard. The Missionary Schools that have actually come up to the standard of Government Colleges are very few ; and when all wholesome rivalry is taken away there is no saying whether the few that have made a fair approach like the Madras Christian College under the guidance of that able and indefatigable Missionary Educationist, the Rev. W. Miller, will not fall back."

(c) Mr. Bickle, Government Inspector of Schools (p. 9 of his evidence) observes :—

" If the Government were to withdraw from the direct management and maintenance of the High Schools and Colleges which they now support, the result, in my opinion, would be their immediate collapse, as I do not believe that a sufficient number of people in affluent circumstances would be found to combine for their maintenance even with a fair share of State aid."

(d) The Revd. T. L. Gallo, S. J., (p. 6 of his evidence) writes :—

" The withdrawal of Government to a large extent from the direct management of schools and colleges relying upon local exertions would have, in my opinion, a very sad effect on the spread of education, for native gentlemen would not be found so devoted to the cause of education. On one hand such gentlemen obtain at present all educational advantages without much trouble or expense to themselves ; and on the other, the elements of public spirit and independence, which alone could make them desirous of relieving Government of this trouble and expense, are certainly not as yet sufficiently developed in this country to allow us to suppose, if Government withdrew from a direct share in the work of education, the balance, which its action now maintains among the other agencies, would not be destroyed. The most powerful agency would gradually obtain the monopoly of education, which might then be easily diverted from its true end, andconverted into a means of extending some private influence, fostering propagandism, &c. Moreover, skill in management, power of organization, long experience, a thorough acquaintance with Western knowledge and Western systems of education, are absolutely essential. There is no doubt that natives are comparatively deficient in these qualities. Should any one object to this that European masters might redeem this inferiority, I would reply, first of all, that native managers would naturally prefer to fill their chairs with native men who would be satisfied with far smaller salaries than Europeans would require, and secondly that it would not be easy to find out European professors to accept office under native control. One might here say that European teachers belonging to European, though private establishments, would perhaps accept the inheritance of Government. The answer obvious to this is that as only Protestant Missionary Societies might be able to do so, there would be great reasons to fear that education would at least run a serious risk of becoming a monopoly in the hands of a class, and thereby the present object of Government education would be easily perverted and changed into engines of propagandism. Add to this that Catholic parents cannot allow their children to receive instruction in schools conducted by Protestant societies where instruction in the various Protestant creeds is given *ex professo*, often made compulsory, and in all cases pervading the whole teaching.

"I cannot in any way doubt that, in the event of the Government withdrawing to a large extent from the direct management of schools and colleges, the standard of instruction would deteriorate, nor could I suggest any measures in order to prevent this result but that which I suggested in the answer to the question 36."

The suggestion made is as follows :—

" The parts that should be taken by Government in a complete scheme of education for India, in my opinion is that Government continue to have a direct share in the work of education, so that Government institutions be allowed to continue as the base of the educational system, give the impulse they have hitherto initiated and directed, and maintain the balance which its action now maintains among the other agencies. As to other agencies, three things are necessary. The first is full liberty to have their own institutions. The second is an impartial distribution of all the assistance in the power of the State. Thirdly, the right to Government of inspecting and controlling their work. I cannot bring myself to believe that any other arrangement might, for the present and very likely, for long henceforth, prove useful to the education in India."

(e) On the same point Mr. Justice Muttusami Iyer in his evidence says :—

(e). " The standard of instruction will certainly deteriorate especially in colleges. The only measure I could suggest to prevent this result is that certain schools and colleges be kept up by the State as model institutions."

Mr. Krishnama Chariar says, in answer to Question 16 :—

"To hand over the few Government institutions to these (Missionary) Societies would, I believe, be, to put it on no higher ground, a grave political blunder. It would lead to deterioration of the quality or a lowering of the standard of high education, and merely hinder the further progress of all education whatever."

Again, he adds at the close of his evidence :—

" The retention, and even the further development, of a few State Secular Colleges as models for the imitation of aided native institutions, as to how the Literature and Science of the West should be taught to Hindu students is, in my opinion, a *sine quâ non*." * * * I am quite sure that if one particle of the efficient support and direct control now extended to the High Education in State Colleges by the Government were withdrawn, not only would the work of Higher Education itself suffer most materially by being scamped and neglected, but the education of the masses would become hopeless."

IX. Christianity, as Christianity, has done nothing more than Hinduism, Buddhism, and Mahomedanism for Education in India, and scepticism is the result of the teaching not of Government, but of Mission Schools.

This is clearly shown in the following extract from a letter which appeared in the *Madras Hindu* of the 7th December 1882, under the signature of *a Hindu Educationist* :—

"What I have principally to do in this letter is to show the baselessness of this *Christian Educationist's* assertion, that scepticism is the fruit of neutral education. But before I proceed to do this, it will be well to let a little daylight in upon one other of his many wonderful propositions. He says in one part of his letter, "our educated friend would never have been an educated man at all, or have troubled his head in the least about morality and truth, if it had not been that God had given to the most Christian country in the world this grand but heathen empire, to christianize and teach the beauty and force of truth and morality ! What has Hinduism, what has Mahommadenism, and what has Buddhism done for his ancestors in this country ?" This, no doubt, is all very triumphant, but what are the facts? India happened to come under the rule of a Christian nation. To administer the government of the country, it was found necessary to throw open all kinds of judicial and executive posts to natives of the country, and to qualify themselves for these Government appointments natives eagerly took advantage, and still do so, of the facilities afforded to them in all classes of schools throughout the country of obtaining the requisite English education. The ambition to obtain a Government appointment, and the fact that this ambition can be gratified only by possessing a good English education, give the true explanation of the success of the several classes of educational institutions in India. Were the Government of India to fulminate an order to-morrow closing these appointments to the natives of the country, every English school from the Himalayas to Cape Comorin might at the same time shut its doors. Education, either for its own sake alone, or for the sake of the concomitant morality that is supposed to go along with it in Mission schools, is not sought for yet by the people of India. Such a state of things may come into existence in the distant future, but it is ridiculous to represent it as having already come, when everyone, except perhaps a perversely blind Christian Educationist, knows the contrary. Christianity, then, has done no more than Hinduism for education in India in the sense in which the *Mail's* correspondent claims that it has done, though a Christian Government has lent a stimulus to it by throwing open the appointments under it to educated men.

"I now come to the question of scepticism. *A Christian Educationist's* position is, " that our so-called neutral education destroys all religion ; and therefore it is idle to talk of morality ; and that the undisputed existence of scepticism is traceable to this cause." The "undisputed existence of scepticism" may be granted to the *Mail's* correspondent, but what the cause of that scepticism is, is quite another question.

" In Mission Institutions the Bible is taught for one hour daily, and in Mission Institutions the fees are considerably lower than in Government Schools. The latter circumstance accounts for the presence of Hindu youths in mission schools, and the former, as a rule, produces one of two very different results, either greater indifference than before, and even hostility, to Christianity, or an unbelief in all religion whatever. Some students who attend the Mission Schools, regard the hour devoted to the reading of the Bible as, though a gratuitous waste of time, a necessary evil to be submitted to in consideration of the saving effected in the matter of school fees. In this frame of mind the Hindu students attend the Bible lesson—present in the body, but absent in the spirit ; and the recollection of the 200 hours or so annually, which, in their opinion, are thus lost from more useful studies, does not certainly increase their love, or lessen their indifference, but rather increases the latter, and, in some minds excites an active antagonism to, Christianity. This, mission-, aries will confess, is not a very desirable result, but it is preferable to what happens in a great many other cases. For, of two contradictories, Christianity and Hinduism, both cannot be true. Accordingly, the other students referred to, find their faith in the beliefs of their fathers unsettled, for to do this is the scope of mission teaching, but they are not prepared to accept the new religion, and they do not accept it, and this of course, leads surely to scepticism, if not to something worse. In Government Schools such a result is impossible. The great moral truths which are common to all religions, and references to which continually recur in the English writers studied, can, in these institutions, be dealt with, and are so dealt with, without raising the suspicion that their enforcement is intended to support one particular form of religion, and to undermine another. *A Christian Educationist* would therefore, so far as the knowledge of every unbiased Hindu goes, be nearer the truth in ascribing " the undisputed existence of scepticism" to the tactics pursued in mission schools, than to the education imparted in Government institutions, where practical morality is inculcated, and where no attempts are made to sap the foundations of all belief.

" What are the Mission schools doing for Christianity ? Nothing is more dreaded in a Mission school, and by a Mission schoolmaster, than a conversion. The Missionaries know that a conversion means the emptying of their schools. A few weeks ago a student in a Mission School wished to be baptized. One of the heads of the Mission was eager that the baptism should take place, but the head of the school, it seems, would have nothing to say to it—on what grounds history does not say. What is the use then of dinning into people's ears what they know to be false? If neutral education produces scepticism, what, in the name of reason, is Mission education doing? Does it produce Christians? No. We have no census returns of the number of sceptics, or atheists, or formalists, or hypocrites, produced by one class of institutions or another, but those who know anything of the country, and of the results of educational efforts in the country, know that scepticism is the out-come, not of Government, but of Mission, schools.

"Missionaries know that conversions at the present time are not noly impolitic but next to impossible, except those popularly known as "rice" conversions. They seem therefore, to think that they may do evil that good may come, and that they may unsettle young men's belief in their faith alleged to be false, in the hope, that in time, they will become Christians. But if these young men do not become Christians, and cease to believe in Hinduism what are they? Sceptics, atheists or whatever name the *Mail's* correspondent prefers; and this class, it is lamentable to think, forms a very large part of the educational out-turn of Mission Schools in India."

X. High Education in India cannot be transferred to Christian Missionary Colleges, if the Government at all care for the feelings and wants of their Native subjects. The following is what Mr. Lethbridge says in chapter VIII of his work on "High Education," and we quote his views *in extenso* as clearly showing the real meaning and motive of the Missionary party in desiring such a transfer, and the serious evils of such a measure :—

"As Christians and as Englishmen we should never forget that the cause of Christian Missions in India has to face a difficulty far greater and more delicate than any that can possibly meet us elsewhere; the difficulty, namely, that by honor, by justice, by every religious sanction, we are forbidden the slightest use of our power as rulers in aid of proselytising efforts. When we forget this—as the "General Council on Education" seems to have forgotten it—we not only commit an unspeakable political blunder, but further than this, we bring the religiou that we would recommend into contempt and hatred. Moreover, such a controversy as that which has been stirred up by the "General Council" makes the position of conscientious Christians in the Indian services particularly disagreeable and invidious. The stern dictates of their highest duty compel them to denounce a movement they would gladly see advanced by other and more straightforward means; and they are thus forced into apparent antagonism to a cause that would be very near their hearts, if it were fairly and honestly advocated. In every way the action of the "General Council on Education" is to be deplored, for the best interests of the people of India, for the sake of the Christian religion and the good name of the English nation, for the credit of our Indian administration. I would fain see the Council alter the line of its advance. The extension of mass education, and the enlargement of the sphere of usefulness of the Missionary Colleges are both excellent objects to be kept in view, if they can be attained fairly and without injury to the State Colleges. Let the "General Council" open subscriptions for these purposes, and the funds so raised will do great good in India both from the immediate results and from the feelings of appreciation and gratitude that will be evoked among the Indian peoples by such a display of disinterested zeal and benevolence. Or let the Council endow some private colleges, so as to enable the latter to compete with the Missionary Colleges on equal terms when the State Colleges are closed. But for any useful action of this kind it is absolutely necessary, first of all, to show clearly that there is not involved in the movement any of that hungering after "hunks of the tempting cake of the education grant" of which the *Hindu Patriot* speaks so bitterly.

"With regard to the suspicion regarding the desire of Christian Missionaries to get the highest education of the country entirely into their own hands, all that need be said is that, whilst the desire is perfectly legitimate and, indeed, praiseworthy on the side of the missionaries, we cannot wonder if orthodox Hindus and Mahommadans do not view the proposal with approval; on the contrary, it is quite reasonable that any disposition on the part of the Government to encourage these proselytising aspirations should be keenly resented by the native community. It is of course obvious that the withdrawal of the Government from the State Colleges will at once enormously increase the power and importance of the Missionary Colleges—and this in several ways. In the first place, the rich endowments which they derive from the home mission funds will make their professors masters of the situation in the competition with "private enterprise." And in the second place, inasmuch as these funds will enable the Missionary Colleges to offer a better, or at any [rate a cheaper, education than that obtainable in the private colleges, the former will be enabled to take up a very different attitude on the question of religious teaching from that hitherto held by them. At present, in the many famous Missionary Colleges of India, the teaching is most efficient in the highest branches of mathematics, of philosophy, of natural science, of the whole " profane" learning of the Universities; but in the matter of religion, General Tremenheere has shown that a little perfunctory Bible reading for perhaps an hour or less each day is all that is ventured on—and it has been stated that the proved conversion of one of the students would probably have the effect of emptying the college to which he belonged. If the parents of the students thought there was any serious risk of their sons becoming Christians they would prefer to pay the Rs. 12 fee of the Government Presidency College rather than incur that risk for the privilege of only paying Rs. 5 per mensem. But in the case we are supposing there would be no Presidency College for them to turn to. The Missionary Colleges would be able to offer their students such an education as would usually place them at the head of the University class-list at an " eleemosynary" rate of payment; and might fairly claim in return the privilege of teaching them freely the doctrines of Christian religion. It is, I admit, difficult for Christian men to recognize in this contingency an unmixed evil. I have felt this difficulty. But every sentiment of fairness and justice must force us entirely to sympathize with and respect the feelings of our Hindu and Mussulman fellow-subjects in demanding from our common Government the most absolute neutrality in religious matters; and as a matter of expediency, as well as of equity, hardly any graver objection could be offered to a Government educational policy than that its natural result would be largely to throw the highest education of the Government into the hands of a propaganda, however laudable the aims of that propaganda might be."

XI. The opponents of State education are merely throwing dust into the eyes of the public in England and in India by entering into various calculations regarding the expenditure on different classes of schools, and leading them to suppose that their figures, which they persistently reprint, are to be relied on, and on this assumption characterizing the action of the educational authorities, in South India especially, as unfair to aided schools in general, and to the

Madras Christian College in particular. But the fact is that the total amount expended on education of all kinds within the Madras Presidency is really considerably less than that given in the Madras Administration Report; but even were the expenditure much greater, Government has pledged itself not to close any of its schools against the expressed wishes of the people to leave the ground clear for the missionaries, and not to desist from doing what is essential to maintain the principle of absolute religious neutrality in employing the people's money for educational purposes.

The *Madras Mail* of the 27th February 1882 contains a well written article entitled "Instructions to the Indian Educational Commission," which, it is an open secret, was written by the ablest and most popular educationist whom Southern India has even seen. The following extract from the article referred to will sufficiently prove the first part of our proposition :—

"The Resolution (constituting the Viceregal Commission) concludes by instructing the Commission to revise the statistical returns of education with the view of placing them upon an intelligible, and uniform basis. This is very desirable. At present it is difficult even for experts to make out the true state of the facts. We had recently occasion to comment on the blunder of adding to the entire cost of Government schools, the refund of the fees, and calling the sum the amount spent on education. But since the date of our remarks, we have observed that the Director's figures have been adopted in the Madras Administration Report, and in the official summary recently reprinted in our own columns. The figure of thirty-one lakhs given as the total sum expended on education from all sources in this Presidency, is swelled by a sum of nearly two lakhs, which is really a refund, and not an additional sum spent on education. The repetition of the blunder requires a repetition of our comment. And, as before, to make the matter clear, we will venture on an illustration. At the Madras Railway station, a person pays Rs. 40 for two railway tickets, one for himself the other for his friend, who is looking after the luggage. As soon as they are quietly settled in their carriage, the friend refunds Rs. 20. Now the Director adds these sums, and says that the tickets cost Rs. 60. There must be some excuse, the reader will say, for perversity of this kind. There is an excuse, and it is this. There was once a time when a part only of the cost of Government schools was paid out of the treasury at the beginning of every month, the remainder being paid out of the fees which were not then credited to the Government, but remained at the disposal of the Director. The total cost was then rightly found by adding the fees to the Government payment, and this system has been continued when the circumstances are entirely changed. One is inclined to exclaim, with how little thought the finances of the Department seem to be managed !"

In support of the latter part of our proposition, we would urge, in addition to what has been already advanced, that those who so violently advocate the abolition of Government schools and Colleges rest their case on the Despatch of 1854. Even this, as Mr. Lethbridge shows, admits of a different interpretation, but there is much stronger, because direct, evidence of the real intent of the Home authorities. In 1857 the Court of Directors in their letter No. 35, dated February 18th, wrote as follows :—" We attach the greatest importance to the system of grants-in-aid *as an auxiliary to the direct measures of our Government* in India, for the extension and improvement of general education." The direct measures were thus to be the backbone of education, and the system of grants-in-aid merely an auxiliary—a very important auxiliary, but still an auxiliary. The Missionaries however say " No : there must be *no* direct Government education :" so that the offspring is to devour its parent.

Again, they would ignore the universal outcry of the Hindu Community against Government severing its direct connection with education : but what says the Secretary of State? He shall speak for himself in his Despatch No. 6, dated 14th May 1862, as follows :—

"It was stated in the Despatch of the Court of Directors of 19th July 1854, that no Government colleges or Schools should be founded for the future, in any district where a sufficient number of institutions exist, capable, with assistance from the State, of supplying the local demand for education ; and it was contemplated that a time might come when many existing Government schools might be discontinued, and the work of education, to a greater extent, carried on by private institutions aided by the State."

" In the application, however, of this latter principle, attention must necessarily be given to local circumstances, and you have learnt from subsequent despatches that *Her Majesty's Government are unwilling that a Government school should be given up in any place where the inhabitants show a marked desire that it should be maintained.*"

On this explicit declaration, the Hindu community may well take its stand. And in so expressing himself, the Secretary of State did but reiterate the intention of the Court of Directors, stated with the same explicitness in their letter to the Government of India, No. 50, dated the 1st April 1857, in the following words.—

"It is alleged that the people of Behar are not likely to accept English instruction except at a Government institution, and . . . we desire that the subject be reconsidered with the view of constituting the school at Dinapore a Government school" (instead of an aided one.)

The Government had a few months earlier in Despatch No. 96 of October 1st. 1856 written—" We approve of the English school at Gowalpara, which had been established and previously maintained by private subscription, having been constituted a Government school."

These declarations distinctly lay down the following principles :—

First.—That there is to be "no abolition or transfer of a Government institution in any place where the inhabitants show a marked desire that it should be maintained."

Second.—That, where circumstances render it desirable, a private school may be constituted a Government one ; just as, in other circumstances, a Government school may be made an aided one.

XII. It is maintained by those who advocate the withdrawal of Government from direct interference with higher education in India, that a large sum would in this way be "set free" for the spread of primary education among the masses,—but this, like all the other missionary propositions, is not true in fact.

We have already shown the want of frankness on the part of the Missionaries in urging the withdrawal of Government from direct connexion with the higher department of education to secure the so-called extension of lower education; but we cannot understand the want of prudence and statesmanship in our rulers in yielding to this pressure from without; nor on financial grounds can we understand their going out of their way to invite the landed gentry and other private agencies to relieve the State, not only of the cost of higher education, but also of the expense of primary education [*vide* the Viceroy's Speech at the last Convocation of the Calcutta University]. It is hard to realize such a strange want of perception of the needs of the country as regards a complete scheme of National Education. The work to be done is one of vital importance to us as a nation, and it should be controlled and paid for by the State, rather than by wealthy landlords and nobles in the country, who are too often liberal against their will, or by the chance donations of pious people in foreign lands, obtained by the missionaries, who are ever ready to beg on the plea of promoting the development of Christianity in India; while everyone here knows the utter failure of Missionary efforts to gain Native youths over to the cause of Christ; and besides the Government should not stoop to seek eleemosynary assistance of this kind, if one of the greatest of its duties is to systematically educate the people. This is peculiarly the case when the government of the country is carried on by foreigners who have great difficulty in ascertaining the indigenuous public opinion indicating national requirements. We would ask our rulers and the religious bodies that persistently agitate and instigate them to change the present educational policy of India, whether, if the education of the people at large in England had waited until their obligation to start and maintain their own schools had been universally accepted, the intellectual advancement in that country would be so marked as it is at present? We challenge the opponents of the present educational plans in India to answer this simple question. Here we will quote the following from an article in the *Madras Mail* of the 27th February 1882 as containing a satisfactory exposition of the views which we know to have commanded the entire sympathy of the intelligent classes of Southern India at the time the article was published—just when the Education Commission was entering on its labours:—

" The burden of the Resolution is primary education. To help those who cannot help themselves, must be the great aim of State aid. Not that Government have any wish to check or hinder higher education ; all they desire is to see the two advance with equal step. If this is all, Madras seems already to have attained the desired result. If we may trust Mr. Grigg's figures, the annual expenditure on elementary education has grown by nine lakhs and a half since 1871, while that on higher and secondary, has increased by less than one lakh, and the total annual account of the former expenditure is now nearly double the latter. With reference therefore to absolute cost, primary education, in this Presidency at least, has already passed its competitor in the race, and is every year leaving it further behind This activity on behalf of primary education is, it must be confessed, recent, and being recent, the entire results under the Despatch of 1854, are much less in that portion of the field than in higher education. And the Government, reviewing the whole period of a quarter of a century, are more impressed with the smallness of the total results, than with the activity of the last decade. In their zeal to rectify this inequality, and not giving due weight to the rapidity with which, as we have seen, it is rapidly rectifying itself, the Government have proposed schemes for the consideration of the Commission, which seem to us for the present to be premature, or which at the least will require very careful consideration, lest in trying to help forward lower education they endanger much that has already been done for the higher.

"One part of the Government scheme is to hand over their own colleges and schools to bodies of native gentlemen, who will undertake to manage them as aided institutions. Not indeed necessarily all at once, so that on a preconcerted day, Government shall wash their hands of all direct connection with education. But all their own institutions are understood to be in the market with the Director as a kind of permanent auctioneer, and the Government declare their willingness to knock them down one after another, whenever a satisfactory bidder comes forward. This is one of the points on which the policy is settled. The Commission is asked merely to assist in the details of the transfer. The natural way of considering a novel scheme of this kind, is first to enquire what is proposed to be gained by it. This is clearly stated by the Government. The object is to *set free* funds now employed on higher and secondary education, with the view of devoting the money thus gained to primary education. But no estimate is given of the amount they hope to gain in this way. We shall endeavour to supply this omission with regard to our own Presidency.

"Every one knows, that for some years past, the annual sum spent on education by the Madras Government out of provincial funds has been between nine and ten lakhs, and if this were the sum to be operated on by the proposed scheme, it would be well worthwhile to run some risk for the sake of the large saving that might be looked for. It will be found, however, on examination, that three-fourths of this sum will be untouched by the proposed abandonment by Government of their schools and colleges, leaving only the remaining one-fourth on which any saving can be made. Out of the sum of between nine and ten lakhs, are paid, first, the expenses of direction and inspection which will still be needed for elementary education and aided education of every kind, and next, the grants-in-aid to private colleges and schools. These two items take in round numbers one-half of the whole. The other half, which is the cost of Government schools and colleges, must be still further reduced before we find the sum we are in search of. For, it includes the cost of normal schools, which must still be kept up by Government, to provide trained masters for aided schools, and the cost of sundry technical schools, such as the Schools of Arts, Agriculture, and Medicine which it is not proposed to drop. Making these reductions, and subtracting also the small amount paid for primary education out of provincial funds, we at last reach the sum of which we have been in quest—that is, the cost of the schools and colleges for higher and secondary education which belong to Government, and which they declare themselves ready to abandon to the highest bidder. That sum is a little under two lakhs and-a-half. This is the entire cost omitting endowments of the schools and colleges just mentioned. But the cost to Government is much less, for there is a refund in the shape of fees to the amount of nearly a lakh and a quarter, leaving the cost to Government about a lakh and a quarter, which would be the amount of saving, if these schools were entirely abandoned. But as the Government propose that they shall be carried on as aided institutions, they will still cost Government the amount of the grant-in-aid. Taking the same proportion of total cost as at present paid to aided institutions of the same class, this contribution will amount to Rs. 70,000. In other words, there will be as the result of this momentous change, a final saving of about half a lakh.

"As the foregoing figures may have been tedious to follow, we shall give a summary of the results in a single sentence. The schools and colleges for higher and secondary education, which the Government are now proposing to abandon, are at present carried on, taking account of the amount refunded in fees, at an annual cost to Government of about a lakh and a quarter. When changed to aided schools, they will still cost the Government Rs. 70,000, leaving a saving of a little more than half a lakh. It is not a great result, and will have no appreciable effect on the education of the masses. Meanwhile, the change will be attended with a certain risk, which it might be worth-while to run for a large saving, but scarcely for a driblet like this. Bodies of native gentlemen ready to give the necessary time and trouble, and willing and able to find the funds required over and above the fees and the grant-in-aid, are not to be had in every town, where there is a Government school. It is true that the Government hope that Municipal bodies will come prominently forward to undertake the management. But most of these are already over-burdened by the duties and expenses which Government have thrown upon them. Besides, it would be unreasonable to charge on a single town, or district, the cost of an institution, which in fact benefits a very much larger area. This remark applies particularly to the case of colleges. Why should the town of Madras bear the expense of the Presidency College which draws its students from every part of the Presidency? Municipal bodies are more-over ill-suited for the management of such an institution. The work is wholly beyond their sphere. To take a single point, they are not in a position to offer such a guarantee as would induce a European Professor to take service under them. But it is unnecessary to argue the question further. It is obvious that in the present stage of native society, neither Municipal bodies, nor groups of independent native gentlemen, offer any hopeful machinery for carrying on the work of the higher education, however well adapted they may be for taking charge of elementary education. The Government suggest no other alternative, but one will immediately suggest itself to every one acquainted with the currents of thought in this Presidency. It is well known that the Missionary bodies in Southern India, have long regarded themselves as the heirs of Government in the matter of higher education. They have often urged Government to retire, and leave the ground clear for themselves. Their opportunity has now come. In the auction which the Government propose, the groups of native gentlemen will not bid. They cannot organize themselves in time. The Municipalities too, will make default. But the Missionary bodies will be eager and forward, and in the end will be left in nearly sole charge of the higher education of the country. Whether this is an agency which offers a reasonable prospect of stability, or whether it is otherwise in every respect desirable, is a question which is well deserving of the attention of the Government and of the community."

In conclusion, we solemnly call upon H. M.'s Government and the Government of India to pause before they adopt, merely to minister to the gratification of the vanity of a body of irresponsible and more or less fanatical agitators, who, no doubt, fancy they are animated by a pure philanthropy, an educational policy which is not only retrograde, but which is calculated to overthrow, not Hinduism, if such be really their desire, but all the superstructure of beneficent results which has been reared on the basis of the enlightened educational policy of the last forty years. Although the Missionary bodies deny that they would accept the charge of Government educational institutions, if Government should retire from direct connexion with education, yet they know well that, were Government schools to be closed to-morrow, there would be practically no educational agencies in the field except themselves. There cannot be two opinions upon this point, and no men of common sense in India would venture to dispute it. Let the Government find out, through proper native channels, what the real wishes and opinions of the people are on this momentous question, before they allow themselves on a false issue—the necessity for the spread of primary education, about which opinion is divided*—to be made parties to the perpetration of a vast iniquity. Let them not readily acquiesce in the wild recommendations of over zealous missionaries, and begin to treat the people of India as slaves who are to have no voice either as to the manner in which, or the agency by which, their children shall be educated, though they have to defray the entire cost of their education. Let them listen to the voice of impartial Anglo-Indian officers who, like the late Political Commissioner, General G. LeGrand Jacob, claim "to know the hidden dangers of Indian political navigation, by intimate acquaintance with the feelings and opinions of its people," having been thrown much amongst all classes of natives and speaking their language as their own. Let them, in short, honestly carry out the Queen's Proclamation which is looked on by the natives as the Magna Charta of their rights, civil and religious. " Firmly relying ourselves on the truths of Christianity, acknowledging with gratitude the solace of religion, we disclaim alike the right and desire to impose our convictions on any of our subjects. We declare it to be our Royal will and pleasure that none be in any wise favoured, none molested or desquieted, by reason of their religious faith or observances, but that all shall alike enjoy the equal impartial protection of the law ; and we do strictly charge and enjoin all those who may be in authority under us, that they abstain from all interference with the religious belief or worship of any of our subjects, on pain of our highest displeasure." So runs Her Majesty's Proclamation of 1858, and who will venture to violate the

---

* *Vide* Evidence of the Bishop of Lahore, and of Mr. Nesfield, Inspector of Schools, Oudh, and also the utterances of the *Hindoo Patriot*, October 16th 1882, and of the *Ress and Ryyyet* of 2nd December 1882.

pledges therein solemnly given ? Yet to induce the Government of India to violate these solemn pledges is the real object of the missionaries and the " Council." In his reply to H. H. the Maharajah of Travancore, Mr. Johnston writes, " The movement originated with men of *pronounced Christian convictions, who desire that all men may share with them in the blessings of the Christian faith*" (Reply, p. 21). In other words, conversion to Christianity is the object of the movement.

It is true that His Excellency Mr. Grant Duff in paragraph 62 of his able review of the events of the past year says that " we may await with the most perfect composure," the report of the Commission, " which is likely to do justice to all parties." We have full trust in the good faith of these words, and also in the good faith of that honest and steadfast friend of the country, Lord Ripon, in appointing the Commission. But neither Lord Ripon nor Mr. Grant Duff knows so well as those who have watched the missionary tactics in India for many years the unscrupulous manner in which, and the questionable means whereby, missionary aims and objects have been effected in India. We do not say that all the Indian Missionaries act thus unfairly, and we certainly have no reason to question the character of the operations of Roman Catholic Missions in this part of India—but we do say that the zeal of a certain proselytising clique of influential Protestant Missionaries has so outrun all discreet bounds that, to a neutral spectator, their actions do appear to be more clever than scrupulous. We do not doubt, we repeat, Mr. Grant Duff's good faith, and we loyally appreciate his honest endeavours to allay the fears of the people of Southern India about higher education—a fear which he confesses to be " a really genuine one." But what we say is, that neither the

Viceroy nor our Governor knows the length to which the missionaries are prepared to go to gain their ends. Mr. Grant Duff, for instance, does not seem to be aware, when he describes Mr. William Miller as a representative of South Indian ideas on educational subjects, that a missionary partisan more one-sided and biased does not breathe than Mr. William Miller. A zealous friend to missionary education he no doubt is ; but he sits in the Commission pledged (Secret Pamphlet, p. 5) to the abolition of State Colleges, he being the foremost of the signatories to a set of answers to the queries, secretly sent out about this time last year by the Reverend James Johnston of London,—signatories who firmly " believe that an honest adherence to the policy of abolition or transference of Government institutions, especially those of the higher class is the one chief measure required to put education in this Presidency on a sound footing," all the time forgetting that the Government Colleges and Schools are nothing less than an organic part of a national system of education in India while the Missionary schools can be nothing more than of temporary value. Mr. Miller, furthermore being the soul of the *Missionary Education Committee* in Madras, has not been, and can never be, accepted as the exponent of Hindu views on education, though he may vainly fancy himself so, and profess to plead the cause of native *aided* schools merely with an eye to serve the interests of *aided* Christian education thereby. Thus Mr. William Miller, instead of being a representative of South Indian ideas, is known to be at heart opposed to the cherished beliefs of the people. Mr. William Miller is not the only one in the Commission who is similarly minded. In these circumstances, it would be a want of moral courage in the educated community of India not to raise its voice, especially when the Viceroy and his Council are anxious to listen to the voice of the people, and warn the Government against accepting any recommendation which would tend to strengthen the hands of those who wish to grind the natives of this country down under an ecclesiastical tyranny.

But, Hindus, equally with the "Council" advocate the carrying out of the Policy laid down by the Home Government—*the whole policy*, let it be noted, and not a part of it. That whole policy cannot be more tersely put than it was by the Secretary of State, in his Despatch to the Government of India, No. 12, of December 24th, 1863, in the following words :—

"Her Majesty's Government have no intention
"of sanctioning a departure from the principles de-
"liberately laid down, and, while they desire that
"the means of obtaining an education calculated to
"fit them for their higher position and responsi-
"bilities should be afforded to the upper classes of
"society in India, they deem it equally incumbent on
"the Government to take, at the same time, all suit-
"able means for extending the benefits of education
"to those classes of the community 'who,' as ob-
"served in the Despatch of July 1854, 'are utterly
"incapable of obtaining any education worthy of
"the name by their own unaided efforts.'"

We would therefore once more repeat that Her Majesty's Government and the Government of India, as well as the Viceregal Commission, must not close their eyes to the real meaning and motive of the missionaries and the "Council" in the mischievous agitation which they have originated and are carrying through with the support of some distinguished statesmen who, though animated by worthy motives, have not had the time to inquire into its true objects. Forty years ago the practice of bazaar-preaching was the only method approved by the missionaries for promoting their views. "When

8

Dr. Duff, after a short experience found that such a method was fruitless, because the ignorance and superstition of the people prevented them from realizing the grandeur of the message, he sought to overcome this obstacle by education. He established schools and gave the pupils a sound secular and religious education, like that which he himself had received at the Parish School in Scotland. At first he met with much opposition. The system was denounced as secular, unchristian, inconsistent with the practice of the early Apostles who went about all the country establishing not schools, but churches."* Influenced by this last consideration, the missionaries did not seek the Government grants in these unsophisticated days, and this more especially because a good deal of the money came from Pagoda funds and was therefore clearly the same as " meat offered unto idols." But by and by, as the grant-in-aid system came into active operation, the grant money, like the money produced by Vespasian's famous tax, was found to smell no worse than other money, their scruples were soothed, and their cry, like that of the daughters of the horse-leech, became " Give, Give." The more they got, the more they wished to get. At last they got so much that Government was compelled to curtail the grants. Then we had the first howl of this agitation, which was to the effect that missionary colleges were being dealt with unfairly by the Educational Department in India as to grants, and that this was nothing less than an attempt on the part of the Department to stamp out all private institutions, meaning their own ; but when it was clearly and triumphantly shown† that such a charge ·

---

* " Christian Colleges as a Missionary Agency" by the Revd. W. A. Lston, Senior Chaplain, Church of Scotland, Madras.

† See the Government Order embodying the correspondence between the Missionaries and Colonel R. M. Macdonald, lately Director of Public Instruction in Madras.

would not hold water, but was ludicrously and gratuitously false—then, " the signal given, behold a wonder ! " another complete change of front takes place ! Ingeniously enough the shriek now became —the ignorance of the masses, the necessity for the spread of primary education,and all the other bunkum of a similar character with which we have been nauseated for a year or more. " Set free," say these philanthropists, "the money now spent by Government on the Higher Education, and devote it to the spread of education among the masses. No harm will come thereby to the Higher Education. No sooner shall the fiat go forth for the annihilation of the Government Colleges than native institutions will spring up in numbers, which, along with the Christian Colleges, both receiving liberal grants from Government, will fully meet all the demands of Higher Education." We have already shown the utterly foundationless character of the assertion as to the springing up of native institutions, and that the withdrawal of Government would simply give a monopoly of the Higher Education to the missionaries ; and that it is this monopoly, and this alone, which they desire, their desingenuous manœuvring and change of front abundantly prove. Somewhat after the manner of Proteus—continually changing—they just now show a new born zeal for the development of Native institutions, which they used to look on with an unfriendly eye, and even oppose and undermine ; but they really do not care two pins for the education of the masses, or for schools of native growth. What they really want is the abolition of State colleges and the affiliation of feeble native institutions to their own, and the diversion thereby of all educational grants into their own hands, ostensibly for educational purposes, but really for pushing forward missionary enterprize and for proselytising India. If Government and the lay section of the Education Commission keep this fact steadily before them, and resolutely adhere to the spirit of the Queen's Proclamation and Her Majesty's solemn assurances as regards any political intermeddling with the civil and religious rights of the people, we have full confidence that they will not lend themselves to carrying out a scheme which would surpass in enormity anything that has yet been recorded in the history of the world.

GOD DEFEND THE RIGHT.